FROM CROW-SCARING TO WESTMINSTER
AN AUTOBIOGRAPHY

BY
GEORGE EDWARDS

FOREWORD

By the
Right Honourable LORD AILWYN OF HONINGHAM, P.C.
(Ex-Minister of Agriculture)
(Chairman of the Norfolk County Council)

Norfolk has produced many men of whom it may be proud and among them is the author of this book.

I am glad to know that his friends have induced Mr. George Edwards to write the story of his life, and it is with great pleasure that I have assented to his request to write a few introductory words, as I have known him for a number of years and been associated with him in a great deal of public work.

On many subjects George Edwards and I may not agree, but on two points at least we are united—in love for Norfolk and in devotion to the interests of agriculture.

Born at Marsham in 1850, the son of a farm worker, George Edwards is a notable example of the way in which adverse circumstances may be overcome by determination and natural ability. The greater part of his life has been devoted to efforts to improve the conditions of the class to which he belongs.

He may, on looking back in the light of experience, reflect—as most men on reaching his age must reflect—that he has made some mistakes, but all who know him[Pg 6] will agree that if he has done so, they have been mistakes of the head and not of the heart.

His honesty of purpose and sincerity of aim, his straightforwardness and conscientiousness, his strong religious principles, are recognized by all who have the pleasure of his acquaintance.

He is a valued member of the Norfolk County Council and a respected Justice of the Peace.

As one of the representatives of Norfolk in the House of Commons, he enjoys the confidence and respect of men of all classes, including many who do not share his political views.

It is with sincere pleasure and the most hearty goodwill that I commend to all who appreciate the record of a strenuous career spent in the pursuit of worthy aims this self-told story of the life of a distinguished Norfolk man.

AILWYN.

August 1922.

INTRODUCTION

This book is more than the record of an adventurous and useful life. It is an outline of the conditions of labour in our greatest national industry during the last seventy years. It is the story of years of struggle to raise the status and standard of life of the agricultural workers of England from a state of feudal serfdom to the relatively high level now reached, mainly through the organization of the Agricultural Labourers' Union. In that long struggle no single person has done more disinterested, solid and self-sacrificing work than my old friend and colleague George Edwards. The Union which he founded some sixteen years ago and in the ranks of which, at the age of seventy-two, he still plays a vigorous and important part, is but the latest fruit of generations of effort at the organization and education of the workers of rural England.

Born in Norfolk in 1850 George Edwards commenced farm work at the age of six. His long life of struggle against tremendous odds should be, and I am certain will be, an encouragement and an inspiration to many whose opportunities and means of social service are greater than his have been. And surely no greater service can be rendered in our time to the cause of national well-being than work devoted to the establishment of labour[Pg 12] conditions in the field of British agriculture in keeping with the vital importance of that great industry.

It would be an unprofitable speculation to try to think of what the author of this book might have achieved had his early life been spent under happier conditions. Poverty, servitude, oppression, the lack of what is regarded as education, as well as the active hostility of those who sought in order to protect their menaced interests to crush him, have all been factors in the life of George Edwards. But in spite of adverse circumstances, and it may be because of adverse circumstances, some men are capable of self-expression and refuse to be conquered. George Edwards is such a man. And he has lived to see tangible results of his life-devotion to the cause of the class to which he belonged.

I think of the author of this book as I met him first, thirty years ago, when he was conducting a campaign on behalf of the persecuted and exploited farm labourers of Norfolk. It is not perhaps easy for those who dwell in towns and cities to appreciate the difficulties that had to be encountered in the conduct of such a campaign; the fear of victimization and perhaps the indifference of those on whose behalf the fight was being waged, as well as the prejudice and hostility of those in authority. It is no exaggeration to say that the man who dared to raise his voice on behalf of the agricultural labourer at that time was in imminent danger of suffering injury to purse and person. A born fighter, George Edwards never counted the cost to himself of his agitations and propagandist activity. Never had any body of workers a more devoted or loyal servant. I have cycled with him,[Pg 13] twenty miles or more, to meetings in various parts of Norfolk, attended by thousands of men, women and children from the surrounding districts, and even in his later years I have listened to him as he spoke with that vigour and enthusiasm and real eloquence which only strong conviction and deep human feeling can command.

Like Arch, his co-worker in the cause of the agricultural labourer, George Edwards inherited his fighting spirit and independence of mind from his mother. And from his wife, in his early manhood, he acquired the rudiments of the elementary education which was to equip him for the business side of his life-work.

A true record of the life of George Edwards would not only be a record of deep human interest on its personal side. He is the most lovable of the many lovable men it has been my privilege to know. But the main public interest and value of this book lies, I think, in the fact that it will give readers a glimpse of the conditions of agricultural England during the last seventy years, and some idea of the ideals and objects of those who have laboured to bring the country worker into line with other workers in the fight for democratic rights and political and economic freedom.

Wellnigh seventy years have passed since George Edwards, the Norfolk farmer's boy of six, entered on his life-work. In that time he has been continually in harness. He is an ex-General Secretary of the Agricultural Labourers' Union. Early in the war period he was elected an alderman of the Norfolk County Council, of which he is a member. He reached in 1920 the goal on which I believe his mind was fixed. In that year he was returned to the House of[Pg 14] Commons as the representative of South Norfolk, the constituency in which a great part of his life had been spent and which he had unsuccessfully contested in 1918. In the House of Commons his contributions to debates on agricultural questions are listened to with the respect they deserve, and I can sincerely say that I share the feeling of all who know him, that George Edwards, O.B.E., M.P., J.P., is not only a worthy representative of the great cause with which he is associated, but a man whom I am proud to count amongst my dearest friends.

WALTER R. SMITH.

[Pg 15]

From Crow-Scaring to Westminster

CHAPTER I
THE HUNGRY FORTIES

In the middle of the nineteenth century there lived in the parish of Marsham, Norfolk, (a little village about ten miles from Norwich and one and a half miles from Aylsham), a couple of poor people by the name of Thomas and Mary Edwards. Thomas Edwards was the second husband of Mary Edwards, whose first husband was Robert Stageman. He died in consumption and left her with three little children to support. In due course she married Thomas Edwards, by whom she had four children, the entire family numbering seven. Thomas Edwards enlisted in His Majesty's Army, served ten years, was sent over to Spain, and fought in the interests of the young Queen Isabel.

In those days a man who had been a soldier was looked upon as being an inefficient workman, no matter what his experience had been before enlistment, and further, he was looked upon by the general public as a rather undesirable character, no matter what his record might have been whilst in the Army, and was considered fit only to be thrown on the scrapheap. Such was the experience of Thomas Edwards.

Before his enlistment he was an experienced agricultural[Pg 16] labourer. Nothing was known against his character and during his ten years' service in His Majesty's Army he bore a most exemplary character. When the Civil War broke out in Spain this country decided to render help to the Queen. Thomas Edwards was sent over with the 60th

Rifles. The war lasted about eighteen months and our troops suffered the greatest privations. Few of the troops returned to tell the tale. Of those that were not killed in action, many died of disease.

These heroes were made to believe that although they were fighting in a foreign country, they were fighting for their own King and Country, and were promised that at the conclusion of the war each man that returned should receive a bounty of £9. This promise was never fulfilled, so far as Thomas Edwards was concerned, nor anyone else so far as he knew.

Thomas, on being discharged from the Army, returned to his native village penniless. The Army pay was only 1s. 1d. per day, and on being discharged he expected that a grateful country would assist him to make a start again in civilian life. But no such good fortune awaited him. On returning to his village he sought to obtain work as an agricultural labourer, but no such employment could he find. For weeks he walked the roads in search of work, but could not find any.

At this period there was a great depression in trade, especially in agriculture. It was in the years 1830 to 1833. It is on record that more than half of the people were receiving poor relief in some shape or form. Bread was 1s. 6d. per 4 lb. loaf. Married men received a wage of 9s. per week, single men 6s. per week. The Guardians adopted a system of supplementary wages by giving meal money according to the number in family, and by so doing enabled the farmers to pay a scandalously low wage. The poor-rate rose to 22s. in the pound, unemployment was most acute. In a large number of villages half the men were without work.

[Pg 17]

Thus this hero, like many others, was workless. The unemployed grew restless and on November 6, 1833, a village meeting was held to demand food. The inhabitants of the parish of Marsham held a meeting which was largely attended, the unemployed turning up in strong force and showing a very threatening attitude. The meeting, however, commenced with the repetition of the Lord's Prayer. Following some very angry words, a resolution was moved demanding work and better wages. To the resolution were added the words: "The labourer is worthy of his hire."

This resolution was moved by Thomas Edwards, and a farmer who was present told him he might go and pluck blackberries again or starve, for he should have no work, and he kept his word.

What this threat meant was soon discovered. My father on his return home penniless, unable to get work, and without food, was forced to pick blackberries from the hedges to eat. One day this particular farmer caught him in his field and ordered him off, telling him he would have no —— tramps in his field picking blackberries.

So insult was added to injustice to this honest man who had fought, he was told, for his country.

Before Christmas in that year he sought shelter in the workhouse, which was then at Buxton. There he remained all the winter. In the following spring he took himself out and got work as a brickmaker.

The summer being over, he obtained employment as a cattle-feeder, but at 1s. per week less than other labourers; and although he had to work seven days, he received the noble sum of 8s. per week. The reason given for paying this low wage was that he had been in the Army and was not an able-bodied workman. No more unjust treatment could be meted out to anyone.

It was in the year of 1840—the year of Queen Victoria's marriage—that Thomas Edwards married the young[Pg 18] widow, Mary Stageman. She had been left with three little children, and had herself been an inmate of the workhouse during her late husband's illness.

The first child born to this couple was a son, whom they named Joseph, the second was named John, and the third was a girl, whom they named Harriet. Between this child and the next to live there was a period of five years. All of this family are now dead with the exception of my sister and myself. As the family increased, their poverty increased. Wages were decreased, and had it not been for the fact that my mother was able to add a little to her husband's wages by hand-loom weaving (which was quite a village industry at that time), the family would have been absolutely starved. Hand-loom weaving was a most sweated industry. One man in the village would go to Norwich and fetch the raw material from the factory and take the finished work back. This weaving was principally done by women, who were paid for it by the piece, that is, so many yards to the piece at so much per piece. A certain sum was deducted to pay the man for the time spent in carrying the work backward and forward to Norwich. If there was any defect in the weaving, then another sum was deducted from the price which should have been paid, and the employers never lost an opportunity of doing this. Poor sweated workers were robbed at every turn.

I have known my mother to be at the loom sixteen hours out of the twenty-four, and for these long hours she would not average more than 4s. a week, and very often less than that.

THE AUTHOR'S BIRTHPLACE, MARSHAM, NORFOLK
THE AUTHOR'S BIRTHPLACE, MARSHAM, NORFOLK.

It was on October 5, 1850, that Mary Edwards bore her last baby boy.

The cottage in which the child was born was a miserable one of but two bedrooms, in which had to sleep father, mother, and six children. At this time my father's wage had been reduced to 7s. per week. The family at[Pg 19] this time was in abject poverty. When lying in bed with the infant the mother's only food was onion gruel. As a result of the bad food, or, properly speaking, the want of food, she was only able to feed the child at her breast a week. After the first week he had to be fed on bread soaked in very poor skimmed milk. As soon as my mother was able to get about again she had to take herself again to the loom, and the child was left during the day to the care of his little sister, who was only five years his senior, and many a shaking did she give him when he cried.

At the christening the parents named the child George, a record of which can be found in the register of the Parish Church, Marsham.

Whether my mother had any presentiment that this child had a career marked out for him different from the rest of the family, I am unable to say, but I sometimes think she had. That this was indeed so has been lately brought to my knowledge.

I have recently revisited the scenes of my childhood days, and met in the village an old man who declares that my mother often said that one day her son George would be a Member of Parliament! What gift of vision this mother must have possessed, for in those days it was never imagined that the doors of Westminster would open to the child of such humble parentage! Her prophecy was partly fulfilled in her lifetime, for she lived to see me a member of a Board of Guardians and Rural District Council, and chairman of the first Parish Council for the village in which I then lived.

At the time of my birth my father was again a bullock feeder, working seven days a week, leaving home in the morning before it was light, and not returning in the evening until it was dark. He never saw his children at this time, except for a little while on the Sunday, as they were always put to bed during the winter months before his return from work. The condition of the[Pg 20] family grew worse, for, although the Corn Laws were repealed in 1849, the price of food did not decrease to any great extent, but wages did go down. Married men's wages were reduced from 9s. to 8s. per week, and single, men's wages from 7s. to 6s. per week. It was the rule in those days that the single men should work for 2s. per week less than the married men. Before the repeal of the Corn Laws had the effect of reducing the cost of living to any great extent, the great Crimean War broke out. This, it will be remembered, was in 1854. Food rose to famine prices. The price of bread went up to 1s. per 4 lb. loaf, sugar to 8d. per lb., tea to 6d. per oz., cheese rose from 7d. per lb. to 1s. 6d. per lb.—in fact, every article of food rose to almost prohibitive figures. The only article of food that did not rise to such a proportionately high figure was meat, but that was an article of food which rarely entered a poor man's home, except a little piece of pork occasionally which would weigh about 1½ lb., and this would have to last a family of nine for a week! Very often this small amount could not be obtained—in fact it can be truly said that in those days meat never entered my father's house more than once or twice a year!

The only thing which did not rise to any great extent was wages. True, able-bodied married men's wages did rise again in Norfolk to 9s. per week. Single men did not share in the rise. My father at this time was taking 8s. per week of seven days.

I was then four years of age, and the hardships of those days will never be erased from my memory. My father's wages were not sufficient to buy bread alone for the family by 4s. per week. My eldest brother Joseph, who was twelve years old, was at work for 1s. 6d. per week, my second brother John, ten years old, was working for 1s. 2d. per week. My sister worked filling bobbins by the aid of a rough hand machine to assist my mother in weaving. My step-brothers apprenticed themselves to the carpentering and joinery trade by the aid of a[Pg 21] little money which was left them by their late father's brother, who died in South America. My other stepbrother went to sea.

In order to save the family from actual starvation my father, night by night, took a few turnips from his master's field. These were boiled by my mother for the children's supper. The bread we had to eat was meal bread of the coarsest kind, and of this we had not half enough.

We children often used to ask this loving mother for another slice of bread, and she, with tears in her eyes, was compelled to say she had no more to give.

As the great war proceeded the condition of the family got worse. My sister and I went to bed early on Saturday nights so that my mother might be able to wash and mend our clothes, and we have them clean and tidy for the Sunday. We had no change of clothes in those days. This work kept my mother up nearly all the Saturday night, but she would be up early on the Sunday morning to get our scanty breakfast ready in time for us to go to Sunday-school.

This was the only schooling I ever had!

From my earliest days, as soon as I could be, I was sent to Sunday-school to receive the teaching of the principles of religion and goodness. My father used to keep our little boots in the best state of repair he could. God alone knows or ever knew how my parents worked and wept and the sufferings and privations they had to undergo. I particularly refer to my mother. I have seen both faint through overwork and the lack of proper food.

I owe all I am and have to my saintly father and mother. It was they who taught me the first principles of righteousness.

[Pg 22]

CHAPTER II
A WAGE EARNER

It was in the year 1855 when I had my first experience of real distress. On my father's return home from work one night he was stopped by a policeman who searched his bag and took from it five turnips, which he was taking home to make his children an evening meal. There was no bread in the house. His wife and children were waiting for him to come home, but he was not allowed to do so.

He was arrested, taken before the magistrates next day, and committed to prison for fourteen days' hard labour for the crime of attempting to feed his children! The experience of that night I shall never forget.

The next morning we were taken into the workhouse, where we were kept all the winter. Although only five years old, I was not allowed to be with my mother.

On my father's release from prison he, of course, had also to come into the workhouse. Being branded as a thief, no farmer would employ him. But was he a thief? I say no, and a thousand times no! A nation that would not allow my father sufficient income to feed his children was responsible for any breach of the law he might have committed.

In the spring my father took us all out of the workhouse and we went back to our home. My father obtained work at brickmaking in the little village of Alby, about seven miles from Marsham. He was away from home all the week, and the pay for his work was 4s. per thousand[Pg 23] bricks made, and he had to turn the clay with which the bricks were made three times. He was, however, by the assistance of one of my brothers, able to bring home to my mother about 13s. per week, which appeared almost a godsend. In the villages during the war hand-loom weaving was brought to a standstill, and thus my mother was unable to add to the family income by her own industry.

On coming out of the workhouse in March 1856 I secured my first job. It consisted of scaring crows from the fields of a farmer close to the house. I was then six years of age, and I was paid 1s. for a seven-day week. My first pay-day made me feel as proud as a duke. On receiving my wage I hastened home, made straight for my mother and gave her the whole shilling. To her I said:

"Mother, this is my money. Now we shall not want bread any more, and you will not have to cry again. You shall always have my money. I will always look after you."

In my childish innocence I thought my shilling would be all she needed. It was not long, however, before I discovered my mistake, but my wage proved a little help to her. I am glad to recall in these days that I did keep my promise to her always to look after her, and my wife had the unspeakable pleasure of taking her to our home, and we looked after her for six years out of my 15s. a week, without receiving a penny from anyone, the Board of Guardians refusing to allow her anything in the nature of poor relief. My wife's mother also lived with us for sixteen years, and died at our house, and for twenty-two years of my married life I maintained these two old people.

My troubles began in the second week of my employment. Having to work long hours, I had to be up very early in the morning, soon after sunrise, and remain in the fields until after sunset. One day, being completely[Pg 24] worn out, I unfortunately fell asleep. Equally unfortunately for me the crows were hungry, and they came on to the field and began to pick the corn. Soon after the farmer arrived on the scene and caught me asleep, and for this crime at six years of age he gave me a severe thrashing, and deducted 2d. from my wage at the end of the week. Thus I had only 10d. to take home to my mother that week. But my mother was too good to scold.

Having finished crow-scaring for that season, I was set looking after the cows, to see that they did not get out of the field, and take them home in the evening to be milked. This I continued to do all the summer.

In 1856, I entered upon my first harvest. During the wheat-cutting I made bonds for the binders. There were no reaping machines in those days, the corn all having to be cut by the scythe. Women were engaged to tie up the corn, and the little boys made bonds with which to tie the corn. For this work I received 3d. per day, or at the rate of 1s. 6d. per week.

When the wheat was carted I led the horse and shouted to the loaders to hold tight when the horse moved. When this work was finished and there was nothing further for me to do, I went gleaning with my mother. In those days it was the custom for the poor to glean the wheatfields after they had been cleared. This was a help to the poor, for it often provided them with a little bread during the winter months, when they would not have had half enough to eat had it not been that they were allowed to glean. The men used to thresh the corn with a flail, dress it and clean it, and send it to the mill to be ground into meal. The rules for gleaning were very amusing. No one was allowed in the field while there was a sheaf of corn there, and at a given hour the farmer would open the gate and remove the sheaf, and shout "All on." If anyone went into the field before this was done the rest would "shake" the corn she had gleaned.

[Pg 25]

This was a happy time for the women and children. At the conclusion of the harvest they would have what was called a gleaners' frolic. In the year to which I am referring, after harvest, I went keeping cows until the autumn, working for a farmer named Thomas Whighten. At the next wheat-sowing I was again put to scaring crows, and when this was finished I was set to work cleaning turnips, and what cold hands I had when the snow was on the ground! And what suffering from backache! Those who know anything about this class of work may judge how hard it was for a child of six and a half years. My mother did all she could to help me. She would get up in the morning and make a little fire over which to boil some water. With this she would soak a little bread and a small piece of butter. This would constitute my breakfast. For dinner I had, day after day for weeks, nothing but two slices of bread, a small piece of cheese, and an apple or an onion.

In the spring I left this employer and went with my father to work in the brickfield for a Mr. John Howlett, the leading farmer, who had about two years before put my father into prison for taking home turnips, but after a time had set him on again. This farmer used to have bricks made in the summer, and my father was set to make them, he having learned this trade when young. In fact, my family for generations were brickmakers as well as agricultural labourers. Being then barely seven years of age, my daily task was made easier by my father, and I had not to go to work until after breakfast. My father, however, had to be up very early, as brickmaking in those days was very hard work. I was just man enough to wheel away eight bricks at a time. The summer being ended, I helped my father to feed bullocks. In the spring of 1858 I again went into the brickfield, and during the following winter was set cleaning turnips by Mr. Howlett. By this time my wages were raised to 2s. per week. Well can I remember the many sore[Pg 26] backs I had given me by the old steward, who never missed an opportunity to thrash me if I did not clean enough turnips. I might say I do not think I ever forgave this old tyrant for his cruelty to me. The treatment I received was no exception to the rule, all poor boys in those days were treated badly. One farmer I knew used to hang the poor boys up by the heels and thrash them on the slightest provocation, and the parents dare not say anything. Had my father complained of the treatment to his son he would have been discharged.

In the spring of 1859 I was set to work as a horseman. This was a new experience to me, but afterwards I was to become an efficient workman, having a liking for horses from the very first. My first job as a horseman was to lead the fore-horse in the drill, and many times the first day the horse trod on my feet. My next job was rolling, and I then thought

I was a man, having for the first time a pair of reins in my hands. This change of work brought me another 6d. a week increase in my wages. By the next spring (1860) I was so far improved that I was set to plough, and on April 7th of that year something happened which caused me to change my employment. The old steward, to whom I have previously referred, rode up by the side of the horses and struck me on the knuckles because I was not ploughing straight enough. I at once swore at him and told him I would pay him out for that treatment when I became a man. He forthwith got down from his horse, took me on his knee, and thrashed me until I was black. I, however, got a little of my own back. I kicked him in the face until he was black, and then ran home and told my mother what had happened. She at once went after the steward, pulled his whiskers and slapped his face. For this she was summoned, and was fined 5s. and costs or fourteen days' hard labour. The fine was paid by a friend.

I soon found another job with a Mr. Charles Jones and rapidly improved in my work. I was kept using horses,[Pg 27] taking a delight in my work, and soon became, although very young, quite an expert in ploughing. The head team-man was a nice fellow, and took a great interest in me, and taught me all he knew about horses. I worked for this man about four years, and then left because he would not pay me more than 2s. 9d. a week! I next went to work for three old bachelors by the names of Needham, William and James Watts, who lived together near to my home. I helped one of them to look after their team of five horses. They also took great interest in me, and here I was taught all kinds of skilled work on the farm, including drilling, stacking and thatching. I worked for them about three years, and by the time I left my wages had risen to about 6s. per week, mother taking 4s. for my board and allowing me 2s. with which to buy clothes and for pocket-money.

I might say by this time the condition of the family had very much improved. My elder brothers had grown up and left home. My mother by her hand-loom weaving had managed to clear off the debts which had been contracted while the children were small. It showed the honesty of these poor people.

I left my work just before harvest because of my employers not being willing to give me enough for my harvest. This was in 1866. I then decided I would leave home. This was the first time my mother chided me for leaving my work, and I have thought since she was right.

I obtained work during the harvest serving the thatcher at Summerfield, near Docking, Norfolk, which was about thirty miles from my home. After harvest I stayed on the farm and looked after the seventh team of horses. A Mr. Freeman had the farm, which was a much larger one than I had ever worked on before. It consisted of 1,000 acres, and one field was 212 acres in extent. The men on the farm did not like me staying. There was a good bit of clannishness about them, and they did not[Pg 28] like people coming from other parts of the county to work in their district.

Hence the men in the other stables did not treat me kindly and often endeavoured to steal my corn. I had, however, been taught a great deal about horses by my eldest brother, who was a stud-groom and well trained in the medical treatment of horses. I was therefore able to treat my horses in such a way that they looked better than any of the others. My employer and the other men did not know my secret, and the latter, not being able to out-do me in this direction, tried to beat me at work. I mention this merely to show the state of ignorance the men were in. In these days, I am happy to say, there is a much better spirit amongst the labourers.

I decided, however, not to stay there more than the year, and on October 11, 1867, I left and returned to my own home. I obtained a job as a team-man with a farmer of the name of Thomas Blyth, at a farm called Botnay Bay. I lived in and received a wage of 2s. per week, with board and lodging, and had to feed and groom five horses. Here I increased my efficiency as a horseman and workman. My employer, though an old tyrant, did put me to all kinds of work. I was set to drill and at the harvest to stack and thatch. The thatching I followed for several years after I left my regular work as a farm hand. I stayed at this place until 1869, when an unhappy affair happened that caused me to leave my farm work for some few years. This farmer had threatened to thrash me and my fellow worker several times. My colleague's name was Sam Spanton. One day when we were at plough he came and accused us of stopping at the end of the field. With an oath I denied this and called him a liar. He thereupon struck me with his clenched fist and knocked me down. As I got up I struck him on the side of the head with my whip-stalk and knocked him down. I at once got on to him and struck him with my fist. My colleague came to my[Pg 29] assistance, and between the two of us, after a rough tussle, we thus far came off victorious, for he never again attempted to hit us. This, however, finished us with this employer. This affair took place in the last week in March 1869, and I obtained work for the summer on a brickfield at Bessingham.

It was, however, a turning-point in my life, greatly to the delight of my mother, for I had begun to adopt rather bad habits whilst in this man's employ. I had taken to snaring hares and catching rabbits and selling them for pocket-money. I had also begun to visit the public-houses, although I never got drunk. This caused my saintly mother some anxious moments.

On leaving this employer I attended a little Primitive Methodist chapel one Sunday evening, when a very earnest lay-preacher, by name Samuel Harrison, was preaching. He took for his text: "How shall we escape, if we neglect so great salvation?" His sermon was a thoroughly orthodox one, and it certainly did appeal to me, and I was led to see I had not been pursuing a right course. I became what we used to call in those days "saved," but which I term now the spiritual forces coming into contact with the forces of evil, which up till then were completely controlling my life, and which, had I not been brought under the influence of the Eternal Spirit at this particular time, might have altered the whole course of my life.

I at once embraced the simple faith of Christ as the Great Saviour of man, although in a rather different light then to what I do now. But I continued to maintain my faith in Christ as the Eternal Son of God, and as the Great Leader and Saviour of men, and in the principles of righteousness advocated by Him as the true solution for all the evils affecting humanity.

I still love my Church, and I remain a loyal supporter of that great section of the Methodist Church, namely the Primitive Methodists, which has during the last[Pg 30] hundred years done so much for the uplifting of the toiling masses of England, and brought light and comfort into thousands of homes. The faith I then embraced created within me new ideals on life and, although an illiterate and uneducated youth, I became very thoughtful and most strict in my habits, thinking I had to give up everything I had hitherto indulged in.

[Pg 31]

CHAPTER III
EDUCATION AT LAST

In the spring of 1870 I went to work in a brickfield at Alby. Here I met a woman who was to play a wonderful part in my future life. Her name was Charlotte Corke, daughter of the late Mr. James Corke of that parish. She herself had felt the pinch of poverty, being the youngest child of nine.

We became engaged, and on June 21, 1872, we married at Alby Church. A record of this event is still to be found in the church register.

At this time I was given a note of liberty by the Aylsham Primitive Methodist Circuit Quarterly Meeting, permitting me to speak in their chapels, and I was appointed to accompany two accredited lay-preachers by the names of Edward Gladden and James Applegate. This continued for two quarters, after which my name appeared on the plan of preachers. In October of the same year I returned to my former employment, agriculture, obtaining a situation with Mr. James Rice of Oulton. I hired a cottage at Oulton, which is near Aylsham (Norfolk), where we lived for the first seven years of our married life. I worked for Mr. Rice for two years, when a dispute arose over the right to stop work for breakfast, and I left and again returned to brickmaking, and went to work at Blickling, about a mile and a half from my home, which distance I walked morning and night. Mr. James Applegate was the contractor and foreman on this yard, on which was manufactured all kinds of ware. My [Pg 32]foreman was quite a skilled tradesman and he took great interest in me and set me to manufacture all kinds of ware, and he also taught me the art of burning the ware. I stayed with him about five years, when, by his assistance, I obtained a situation as brick-burner with a Mr. John Cook of Thwaite Hall and, on October 11, 1879, I moved to Alby Hill into one of my employer's cottages.

The September Quarterly Meeting of 1872 of the Aylsham Primitive Methodist Circuit decided that my name should appear on the preachers' plan as an "Exhorter," and I was planned to take my first service on the third Sunday in October of that year.

Up to this time I could not read, I merely knew my letters, but I set myself to work. My dear wife came to my rescue and undertook to teach me to read. For the purposes of this first service she helped me to commit three hymns to memory and also the first chapter of the Gospel according to St. John. It was a big task, but she accomplished it, and this is how it was done. When I returned home from work after tea she would get the hymn-book, read the lines out, and I would repeat them after her. This was repeated until I had committed the whole hymn to memory.

MR. AND MRS. EDWARDS'S FIRST HOME AFTER MARRIAGE, OULTON-NEXT-AYLSHAM, NORFOLK
MR. AND MRS. EDWARDS'S FIRST HOME AFTER MARRIAGE, OULTON-NEXT-AYLSHAM, NORFOLK.

My first three were good old Primitive Methodist hymns. The opening verse of the first hymn I learned was:—

Hark, the Gospel news is sounding,
Christ has suffered on the tree.
Streams of mercy are abounding,
Grace for all is rich and free.
Now, poor sinner,
Look to Him who died for thee.
The second hymn was:—

There is a fountain filled with blood,
Drawn from Immanuel's veins;
And sinners plunged beneath that flood,
Lose all their guilty stains.
[Pg 33]

The third hymn was:—

Stop, poor sinner, stop and think
Before you further go.
Will you sport upon the brink
Of everlasting woe?
On the verge of ruin stop,
Now the friendly warning take,
Stay your footsteps or you'll drop
Into the burning lake.

The last hymn does not appear in the present-day Primitive Methodist hymnal. Needless to say, I have long ceased to use the hymn. It was too horrible for my humanitarian spirit. I might say that at my first service I was not quite sure that I held the book the right way up, as I was not quite certain of the figures. I had, however, committed the hymns to memory correctly, and also the lesson, and I made no mistakes. In those days we used to give out the hymns two lines at a time, as very few people could read, and they could possibly remember the two lines. There was no musical instrument in many of the small village chapels at that time. My wife went with me to my first appointment and listened. My first text was taken from the first chapter of John: "Behold the Lamb of God which taketh away the sin of the world." I would not like to say the sermon was a very intellectual one. It was, however, well thought out as far as my limited knowledge would allow me to do so, and in preparing it I had the assistance of my wife. We had spent nights in thinking it out, and it certainly was orthodox in the extreme. I made rapid progress with my education under the tutorship of my wife, who would sit up very late at night to teach me. She would sit on one side of the fireplace and I on the other. I would spell out the words and she would tell me their pronunciation.

By the time the next plan came out I could just manage to read my lesson and hymns, but not until I[Pg 34] had gone through them many times with my wife and had mistakes rectified.

One interesting little incident occurred about this time. I went to an appointment one Sunday about eight miles from my home. A brother lay-preacher was planned at the chapel in an adjoining village, hence we travelled most of the way together. Coming home it was very dark, and we had to travel some distance by a footpath across some meadows. We lost ourselves! I told my companion to follow me, but it turned out that it was a case of the blind leading the blind, for no sooner had I instructed my companion than we both walked into a ditch up to our knees in water, and had to walk the rest of the way home with wet feet! This was not the day of bicycles nor yet horse-hire. The circuit to which I was attached was very large, and for many years I walked sixteen miles on the Sunday, conducted two services, and reached home at eleven o'clock at night. Whatever may have been our weaknesses in those days, it must be admitted we were enthusiastic and devoted to the cause we advocated. No sacrifice was too great.

Having once learned to read, I became eager for knowledge. Until then I possessed only a Bible and hymn-book and two spelling-books. But I had no money to buy other books. My wife and I talked it over, and I decided I would give up smoking and purchase books with the money saved. I was then smoking 2 oz. of tobacco a week, which in those days cost 6d. This did not seem much, but it was £1 6s. a year. It was a great sacrifice to me to give up smoking, for I did enjoy my pipe. I had, however, a thirst for knowledge, and no sacrifice was too great to satisfy my longing. My first purchase was Johnson's Dictionary, two volumes of The Lay-preacher, which contained outlines of sermons, Harvey's Meditations among the Tombs and Contemplation of the Starry Heavens, a Bible dictionary, and a [Pg 35]History of Rome. These I bought second-hand from Mr. James Applegate, who was a great reader. The Lay-preacher I used extensively for some years, and it certainly did help me for the first few years. I ultimately discarded the two volumes and relied upon my own resources, and I should advise every young man with the advantage of education, who is thinking of engaging in such great and good work, never to use such books, for it is far better for him to think out subjects for himself and store his mind well with knowledge.

The different Primitive Methodist services of my early days would be out of date now, and the quaint sayings of those days, though effective then, would cause some amount of amusement to our young educated folk of to-day. One form of service was called a "love-feast," at which small pieces of bread were taken round with water. The meeting was thrown open for anyone to speak, and then the simple, faithful, uneducated, saintly people, in relating what to them was Christian experience, would express themselves in peculiar phrases. I call to mind the statement made by a brother at one meeting who said he felt "like a fool in a fair." At the same meeting another said he thanked God that although that was the first time he had attempted to speak, he was getting used to it. Others would relate what dreadful characters they had been and what religion had done for them.

Although my preaching efforts did not give me entire satisfaction, still I can look back with pleasure at some of the results of my labours. Although uneducated and not well informed and although I used such phrases and put the Gospel in such a way that I should not think for one moment of doing to-day, still it had its effect. I can recall instances of ten and twelve of my hearers at my Sunday services making a stand for righteousness. Many of them in after years became stalwarts for truth.

They also soon began to be dissatisfied with the conditions[Pg 36] under which they worked and lived. Seeing no hope of any improvement they migrated to the North of England, and found work in the coalfields, and never returned to their native county. When in Newcastle last December I met several of my old converts and friends.

With my study of theology, I soon began to realize that the social conditions of the people were not as God intended they should be. The gross injustices meted out to my parents and the terrible sufferings I had undergone in my boyhood burnt themselves into my soul like a hot iron.

Many a time did I vow I would do something to better the conditions of my class.

[Pg 37]

CHAPTER IV
PIONEERS AND VICTIMS

The year 1872 will throughout history be considered the most interesting period from the standpoint of the agricultural labourers of England. There had been some improvement in the condition of the labourers of England through the increase of the purchasing power of their wages, largely due to the abolition of the wicked Corn Laws and the adoption of Free Trade. Moreover, agriculture was never more prosperous than it was from 1849 to 1872. But, despite the increase in the purchasing power of the labourers' wage, the condition of the workers had not improved at the same rate as agriculture had improved. The working hours were as long as they had been for the preceding hundred years, the labourers were no more free to bargain with their employers than their fathers had been for fifty years before, and there was much discontent. In fact, the whole countryside was seething with discontent and we were much nearer a serious upheaval than many people thought. The farmers were arrogant and oppressive, and the gulf between the farmer and the labourer was greater than ever before. The labourer had acquired a little knowledge and the town workers were uprising. Many of the sons of the labourers who had left agriculture since 1864, being disgusted with the low wages of the labourer, had sent glowing accounts over to their friends, and a great migration had again set in until very few young men were left in the villages.

[Pg 38]

Early in the year 1872 a few labourers met in the village inn at Barford, in Warwickshire, and decided to make an effort to form a Union. But they were without a leader, and it was in search of such a person that they turned their attention to Mr. Joseph Arch, who was a Primitive Methodist lay-preacher. They waited upon him at his residence and informed him that they wanted to form a Union for the agricultural labourers and asked him if he would lead them. Mr. Arch hesitated for a time, as his clear vision could discern that it would cause a tremendous upheaval and he was not sure of his class. After due thought, and through the persuasive powers of Mrs. Arch, he ultimately consented. Accordingly it was arranged that a meeting should be held under what is now known as the Welbourne Tree.

This meeting was attended by at least two thousand agricultural labourers from all parts of the country, and it was there decided to form a Union. The news of the meeting spread rapidly throughout the country. All the newspapers gave it prominence with such headlines as "The Uprising of the Agricultural Labourer." Numerous meetings were held in various parts of the country, and in the second week in May a meeting was held on the children's playground at Alby where I was at work. This was a month before my marriage. I attended the meeting. It was addressed by a local preacher, who was an agricultural labourer, named Josiah Mills, and by Mr. Burton from Cromer. I also spoke, although, as stated before, I could not read. Still, I related my experience of how I was obliged to go to work at the age of six.

A branch of the Union was formed and I became a member. But, as Mr. Arch had foreseen, trouble soon arose, for this new movement met with the most bitter opposition.

Labourers were discharged by the hundred. It was evident that the farmers were bent on crushing the [Pg 39]movement in its infancy. Many labourers who lived in their employers' cottages were victimized and turned out into the road. One case which personally came to my notice was that of a poor man and his wife and family who were turned out on to the road with all their furniture and a friendly publican took them in. Scores of farmers locked their men out because they would not give up their Union cards.

This threw Mr. Arch on to his beam ends, as he and his men had no previous knowledge of Trade Unionism. Happily for him and the movement generally a leading Trade Unionist by the name of Mr. Henry Taylor paid Arch a visit and offered him all the help possible. This brought help from other Trade Unionists.

In Norfolk we were specially favoured, as the proprietors of the Norfolk News and the Norwich Mercury (the latter one of the country's earliest newspapers) opened the columns of the Eastern Weekly Press and the Peoples' Weekly Journal respectively to Labour news. Thus the news of the Union spread rapidly and the story was told of the uprising of the agricultural labourer. Hundreds of meetings were held in Norfolk as well as in other counties, branches of the Union were formed everywhere, and within six months 150,000 labourers had joined some Union. It must be remarked that in the first six months the branches formed were all independent Unions.

During the summer Arch, with the help of Mr. Taylor, drew up a list of rules and called a conference of the branches formed in the Warwick district, at which it was decided to form a National Union, its central office to be at Leamington. Mr. Arch was elected President and was sent on a mission throughout the country to explain the rules. Arch soon gathered around him a number of persons who were prominent in the political world, including the late Sir Charles Dilke, Howard Evans, John Bright, George Mitchell, and a host of others.[Pg 40] Among those in Norfolk who rallied to Arch were the late Mr. Z. Walker, who remained a faithful follower to the end, the late Mr. Lane of

Swaffham, the late Mr. Colman, the late Mr. George Rix, and Mr. George Pilgrim. But all the branches did not join with Mr. Arch. Kent and Sussex formed a Union of their own, which became very strong in those two counties. Lincolnshire also formed a Union and it became known as the "Lincolnshire Amalgamated Labour League." A Mr. Banks became its General Secretary. This Union gained considerable support in Norfolk and had several strong branches in the county, and among its warm supporters were the late Mr. James Applegate of Aylsham, the late Mr. James Ling of Cromer and Mr. James Dennis of Hempton.

All these Unions grew in strength, but unfortunately a spirit of rivalry grew up between them and much mischief was done.

My first acquaintance with Arch was at Aylsham in September 1872, when he came over to explain the code of rules drawn up by the Warwickshire Committee and to invite the branch there to join the Union. The meeting was held in Aylsham Town Hall, which was packed. All in the audience were, however, not in sympathy with the movement. There were several farmers present.

One farmer asked Arch if his mother knew he was out?

Quick as lightning came the retort: "Yes," replied Arch, "and she sent me out to buy a fool. Are you for sale?"

That was just such an answer as the farmer who asked the foolish question deserved. He had, however, no further opportunity of asking questions, for he was soon roughly handled and was promptly thrown out of the hall.

There were many strikes and lock-outs during the first[Pg 41] nine months of this uprising of the labourers. The greatest opposition was raised by the farmers.

I was involved in a strike in the first year of the Union's existence. Although only just twenty-two years of age and recently married and unable to read, I became greatly interested in the movement and never lost a chance of attending a Union meeting.

The first general demand we made for an increase in wages took place in March 1873. We asked that wages should be increased from 11s. to 13s. a week, so far as Norfolk was concerned, and this demand was granted. It had never reached that figure before. This gave a great stimulus to the movement generally. The Aylsham branch of which I was a member decided not to join Arch's Union, but joined the Lincolnshire Amalgamated League, which governed on the principle of each district holding its own funds and paying a quarterly levy to the central fund, on the same principle which obtained with the Oddfellows and Foresters Friendly Societies. The next great struggle was in the spring of 1874, when a demand was made for another 2s. increase and time off for breakfast. Up to that time we were not allowed to stop for breakfast, and we had no food from tea-time the previous day until dinner-time the next day. Many farmers allowed the concession but others would not. The man I worked for at Oulton, Mr. James Rice, was one of the latter, although a member and a deacon of the Congregational Church in that village. We adopted all kinds of methods to snatch time to eat our piece of bread. Scores of times I have held the plough with one hand and eaten the bread with the other. Others, when a number were working together, would set one to watch to see if the boss came while they ate their bread.

This demand was hotly contested and I became involved and struck work. Fortunately for me I had another trade at my back, namely brickmaking. There was a[Pg 42] great call for brickmakers at this time and I obtained work at once with James Applegate at Blickling, himself a leader of the Amalgamated Labour League, so I had not to call on the funds of the Union at all and I did not go back to farm work for several years. During these two years I had made rapid progress with my education, and I was so far advanced that I could begin to read a newspaper. I had, however, not been in ignorance of happenings in the world around me, for my wife had always read to me the weekly papers. The first newspapers I read were the Eastern Weekly Press and the People's Weekly Journal, the two local papers. I had, however, not spoken at a Labour meeting since the first meeting was held two years before, but I had been on the preachers' plan for two years and had begun to have a little confidence in myself. I at once begun to speak at local labour meetings.

The strike going on at this time was successful, and the village labourer in Norfolk for the first time in his history received his 2s. 6d. per day and the right to stop for breakfast.

But the great struggle began as soon as this was settled. The farmers of Suffolk at once locked their men out, not on the question of wages, but because the men would not give up their Union cards. Some four thousand men were locked out and thrown on to the funds of the various Unions. Arch and others visited the large centres of industry and over £20,000 was collected for the funds. Religious services were held on the Sundays and spiritual addresses given. I at once threw myself into this kind of work, although only a young man of twenty-four years of age, and in the village in which I then lived, Oulton, I preached my first Labour sermons. My soul burned with indignation at the gross cruelty inflicted on my parents and the hardships I had undergone, and I became determined to fulfil the vow I had made when quite a lad, namely, to do all I could to alter the conditions under[Pg 43] which the labourers lived. I was, however, most anxious to ensure myself that I was doing the right thing from a religious point of view, and again by the assistance of my dear wife I searched the Scriptures and soon was able to satisfy myself I was doing the right thing. Then, as now, to me the Labour movement was a most sacred thing and, try how one may, one cannot divorce Labour from religion.

I found work when the strike took place with Mr. James Applegate, who was many years my senior and himself a leader in the Labour League and an advanced politician, although he possessed no vote. He had posted himself up in Radical politics, for in those days we only knew two political parties. Anyway, I had a real political schoolmaster, and my first political lessons were of the Liberal school of thought. I set myself to work hard in the study of political questions and got possessed of every scrap of political information. My means would not allow me to purchase literature, but I soon became a most ardent Liberal.

Soon after the great struggle of 1874 the labourers began to lose interest in the various Unions. Many of the young men again left the villages and either migrated to the North of England or emigrated to America. I still kept up my political studies and at the same time, by the assistance of Mr. Applegate, I became skilled in the work in which I was then engaged. I kept with Mr. Applegate for five years.

It was in 1880 that my father died.

In October 1879 I obtained a situation with the late Mr. John Cook of Thwaite Hall as brickmaker and burner, and moved into part of an old farmhouse at Alby Hill. One of the conditions of employment was that I should take the work by contract; that I should raise the earth, make the bricks and burn them at 10s. per thousand, the employer finding all tools and coal for[Pg 44] burning. Further, whilst I was not so engaged he was to find me work as a farm labourer. I also undertook to do my harvest on the farm. On leaving Oulton I was out of the reach of the Union to which I then belonged.

I then joined Arch's Union and became an active member. I got along very well with my employer for some few years, but in 1885 an agitation arose for the granting of the franchise to the agricultural labourers and all rural workers. I at once threw myself into the movement and spoke at many meetings. I had become fairly well educated by this time by hard study. I was, however, laying up in store for myself some serious trouble, for my employer was a bigoted Tory.

The franchise was introduced into the House of Commons by Mr. Gladstone, who was then Prime Minister, and was met with bitter opposition by the Conservatives. As stated previously, a great campaign was commenced in which I took a leading part, this greatly enraging the local Tories. After my speech at a meeting one night in March 1895 my employer came to me at my work and in a most autocratic manner said he had been informed that I had been speaking at some Liberal meetings and demanded to know if this was true? I at once replied that it was true. His reply to that was that if I wished to remain a man of his I should have to give that kind of thing up, for he would not have any man of his attending such meetings, setting class against class. The fighting spirit that I inherited from my mother at once rose and I replied in dignified language that much as I respected him as an employer, I respected my liberty a great deal more and could not on any condition comply with his request. Further, I considered so long as I did my work satisfactorily and did not neglect it in any way and led an honest and straightforward life, neither he nor anyone else had any right to dictate how I spent my evenings. I should therefore claim my liberty as a citizen. He had no arguments to use against this, but said I would[Pg 45] have to leave. It was then that my spirit of independence was put to the test. I was not long in deciding, and I told him at once I should take his notice, for my whole soul revolted against such tyranny. This seemed to stagger him, for it was the first time his authority had been challenged in such a way. As soon as he had time to recover himself, he asked when I wished the notice to expire. I told him not until I had finished my contract, for I had already raised sufficient earth to make 100,000 bricks and I should complete that before I left. He insisted that he would force me to leave at once. I told him to try and put the threat into execution and I would sue him for breach of contract. Again he was completely taken back and asked me if I meant it? I told him I did and defied him to break the contract. He at once saw he was in the wrong and said: "Very well, finish your contract." I replied that I intended to and then he could carry out his threat. Being thwarted in this direction he thought he would hit me in another way.

My wife's mother was a widow and was living with me. The Guardians allowed her 2s. 6d. per week. My employer was a member of that Board, which at once took 6d. a week off her relief. My victimization was made known throughout the country. I at once informed the leaders of the Union, and also the Liberal Party, and this act of political tyranny was denounced on every Liberal and Labour platform. Coming at a time when the labourers were about to be enfranchised it caused quite a stir in the country.

I was offered by the Liberals an organizing and lecturing position, but this I declined, as, having insisted upon finishing my contract, I did not intend giving the Tories an opportunity to say I had broken it. Further, I had no wish to give up manual labour, nor had I confidence in myself that I could do the work. I felt I was not sufficiently educated or well informed to do that[Pg 46] kind of work; thus I kept at my brickmaking. Into this I put more energy than I think I had ever done before. It was a fine season and I was able to turn out a better class of brick than in previous seasons. At the same time I attended as many political meetings in the evenings as I could and I also read every bit of literature I could get hold of.

During the summer the Franchise Bill, coupled with a Redistribution Bill, was passed, and for the first time in English history the agricultural labourers were enfranchised. Norfolk was mapped out into six single-member rural constituencies. Where I lived became known as North Norfolk. It became evident that there would be a General Election in November, and that by the time I had finished my contract the election would be near. This the leading Tories appeared to advise my employer would put him into a very awkward position, for he had not only given me notice to leave my employment, but also my house on October 11th. Hence he came to me in July and said he wished to withdraw both notices and wished all misunderstanding to cease. After consultation with some of my friends I accepted the offer. I was, however, never satisfied, although the offer to withdraw the notices was genuine as the following correspondence will show.

In July I received the following letter from the late Mr. Charles Louis Buxton, who was the then leader of the Liberal Party in North Norfolk:—

Bolwick Hall, Aylsham,
July 20, 1885.

Dear Mr. Edwards,

I was delighted to hear yesterday that your employer had withdrawn his notice for you to leave your work and house, and hope everything will go on smoothly and that you will be quite happy and that we shall have no more of this kind of victimization,

Yours truly,

C. L. Buxton.

I replied as follows:—

Charles Louis Buxton, Esq., J.P.
  Bolwick Hall, Aylsham.

Dear Sir,

I thank you for yours of the 20th re my employment. I must confess I do not derive the same satisfaction from the withdrawal of the notice as you appear to do. Although it was withdrawn unconditionally, each of us to be free to go our own way, I feel convinced when the election is over he will find some excuse to get rid of me.

Nevertheless, I will stand by my principles, come what may.

Yours sincerely,

George Edwards.

I finished my season's work fairly early, and I think I earned more money than I had ever done before. Having finished my season's work, I returned to my farm work as before.

In October the election started in all earnestness. For three weeks I addressed six meetings a week. This I might say was all voluntary work, as I kept at my daily employment all the time, being determined not to absent myself from work one hour.

Mr. Herbert Cozens-Hardy, who afterwards became Lord Cozens-Hardy, Master of the Rolls, and whose son and heir was in after years by a strange coincidence to be my opponent in my first bid for parliamentary honours, was chosen Liberal candidate for North Norfolk. Mr. Joseph Arch was selected Liberal and Labour candidate for North-West Norfolk, Mr. Robert Gurdon was chosen Liberal candidate for Mid-Norfolk, Sir William Brampton Gurdon for South-West Norfolk, and a Mr. Falk for East Norfolk. After a most hotly contested election, Mr. Cozens-Hardy beat his opponent, Sir Samuel Hoare, by over 1,700 majority. Mr. Arch and Mr. Robert Gurdon were also elected by good majorities, whilst Sir Brampton Gurdon and Mr. Falk were defeated.

The election being over, things quieted down and, so far as I was concerned, nothing untoward happened. My employer and myself appeared to be on very good terms. Early in the new year, 1886, when I asked him for my orders as usual, he informed me that he should not make any bricks that year, as there were a good many standing on the ground and there was not much sale for them. As a matter of fact there were not many bricks on the ground, not so many by 20,000 as there were the year before when he gave me the order to make 100,000 and, further, when there was a prospect of a greater sale than in the previous year. A few weeks later I received notice to leave the farm work, and on April 6th I was served with another six months' notice to leave my cottage. Thus the fear I had expressed to Mr. Buxton nine months before became true, and proved that he only withdrew the previous notice to save himself from the law against intimidation.

I obtained work for the season's brickmaking with Mr. Emery at Stibbard. Strange to relate, before my notice expired to leave the cottage, my landlord and late employer died. He had not been dead more than a month before his brother, Mr. Herbert Cook, who was heir to the estate, called at my house in my absence and informed my wife that he should carry out his brother's notice. Now came the difficulty of getting another house, and it looked for some time as if I should go homeless. I first hired a cottage at Colby on the Gunton estate, but before I could move into it it was let with the farm, and of course, being an agitator, I could not have it. Thus within a few weeks of October 11th I had no prospect of a home. It was then that a friend came along in the person of Mr. Horace Car, who lived at Wickmere. He had hired a little farm in another village and did not want his cottage at Wickmere and sub-let it to me.

The election of 1885 was doomed not to stand long. Mr. Gladstone introduced his Irish Home Rule Bill,[Pg 49] which caused a terrible split in the ranks of the Liberal Party, and in July 1886 the Government was defeated and a General Election took place. Mr. Cozens-Hardy again came forward. This time his opponent was Mr. Ailwyn Fellowes, now Lord Ailwyn of Honingham, a gentleman whom I hold in the highest esteem and who has done me the honour of writing a foreword to this book. Mr. Arch was this time fought by Lord Henry Bentinck, who defeated him by twenty votes. At this election I was brought a great deal into Mr. Arch's company whilst working in his division. I attended several of his meetings and spoke for him. I remember being with him at one meeting during the election when we spoke from a wagon standing close to a pond. During the proceedings a young farmer rode into the company and endeavoured to strike at Arch with his whip-stalk. No sooner did he do this than he was unhorsed and ducked in the pond, greatly to his discomfort. This, I should think, he never forgot.

Mr. Arch and I were destined in after years to work together in one common cause, although, unfortunately, we were to belong to two different Unions. Most of the meetings I attended in this election were in my division and, smarting under the gross injustice that had been meted out to me, I spoke out very strongly. My victimization had created a bitter feeling in the division, and some very exciting scenes occurred during the election. At one of these meetings, after being interrupted by one or two of the most ignorant Tory farmers, I prophesied that after the election the Tory political victimisers would be politically dead and on their political tombstone would be written the following epitaph:—

Here lay the Party that never did any good
and, if they had lived, they never would.

This naturally caused a great deal of laughter, but my enthusiasm for the cause I then believed to be right[Pg 50] had somewhat blinded me to the fact that the wheels of human progress move very slowly and that my whole life would have to be spent before Democracy would come into its own. Let me remark that fate sometimes seems to be cruel. It was the son of the very man on whose behalf I suffered so much and for whom I worked so hard to secure his return at least in three elections who fought me in after years in South Norfolk when I stood for Parliament the first time! I thought at the time it was rather an ungracious act.

Well, this election went badly for the Liberals in the country and the Tories were returned to power with a majority of 100.

Some hard times were in store for me. At the end of the season my work at Stibbard also ended. I moved to Wickmere, but no one in the district would employ me, although I was an efficient workman. I was a horrible Radical, setting class against class! Strange to relate, in those days the Liberals were looked upon as being out for destruction. To be a Liberal was looked upon as belonging to a most discreditable party. They were classed as infidels, wanting to pull down Church and State, and disloyal to Queen and Country.

To-day the same things are said about the Labour Party. We of the Party are called all kinds of names. But those who make the statements know they are untrue.

I tried everywhere to get employment, but none could I find.

At last Mr. Ketton of Felbrigg Hall offered to find me work on his home farm, but he had no cottage to offer me. Felbrigg was six miles from Wickmere. I accepted the employment and for eighteen months or more I walked night and morning this six miles, a journey of twelve miles every day! Whilst living here my wife's mother died. I had kept her for sixteen years, her only income being parish relief. In 1878 Mr. Ketton found[Pg 51] me a cottage at Aylmerton and I settled down comfortably once again as a farm labourer.

At this time agriculture was sorely depressed. The labourer's wage was rapidly being reduced and reached the miserably low figure of 10s. per week, and in some districts 9s. per week. The labourers had left their Unions and were in a most helpless position. This was brought about by many causes, one being the great falling out amongst the leaders. Arch had the misfortune to fall out with all his best supporters. Mr. Henry Taylor resigned his position as General Secretary. Mr. Howard Evans and Mr. George Mitchell had left him. Mr. George Rix of Swanton Morley had resigned, and he took with him a large district and formed a Union which he called the Federal Union. In fact, in every county, with the exception of Norfolk, the Unions became defunct. The Kent and Sussex Union went smash, the Lincolnshire and Amalgamated Labour League became defunct, and all that remained of Arch's Union were a few members belonging to the sick benefit department, the funds of which were being fast depleted.

Under these circumstances the political power placed in the hands of the labourers but further enslaved them and made them easy victims for the Tory party. Happily for me I had at last got under a Liberal employer, who not only was favourable to the men, but showed his sympathy with them by paying them 1s. per week above the rate paid by other employers, and I was able to breathe freely without any fear of victimization. My employer also assisted me by lending me books and papers on political problems. He also put every kind of work on the farm in my way to enable me to earn extra money. I at once settled down to study even more closely than I had done before. Thirsting for knowledge, religious, social and political, I set about adding to my library. I became a close student of theology and took great interest in many of the theological subjects which were[Pg 52] disturbing the Christian world at that period, such as the doctrine of eternal punishment, and I soon became what was known then as a Liberal in theology. When I purchased a new book, I never read any other until I had read it through and thought the matter out for myself. I never accepted a thing as a fact just because someone else said it was so. Included in the new works I bought at this time were Canon Farrar's Life of Christ, the same author's Eternal Hope, Dr. Dale's work on Conditional Immortality, Mr. Robertson's book entitled Eternal Punishment, not Eternal Torments. I also read very closely Dr. Parker's books. Taking the other side, I also became a regular reader of the weekly periodical the Christian Commonwealth, which was published about this time to counteract what they termed the heterodoxy of the Christian World. Strange to say, this paper became a thousand times more heterodox than the Christian World ever could be, for it became a strong advocate of the Rev. R. J. Campbell's New Theology.

My close study of these matters marked me out for trouble. In fact, Job's description of man seemed to apply to me in every respect, for I seemed to be born to trouble as the sparks fly upward. I was called up before the Quarterly Meeting of my Church for what some of the elder brethren termed heterodoxical preaching and I was regarded as almost an infidel. Never, however, was a more false accusation made against anyone, for my faith in the eternal Truths was never stronger. But I had a strong supporter in my friend Mr. James Applegate, who himself was a progressive in thought, and the matter blew over and I was left to go on in my own way.

At this time there was a deal of discussion on the Single Tax Movement as advocated by Henry George. I became interested in this and purchased his books on social problems, Protection or Free Trade, Progress and Poverty and The Condition of Labour. These I closely read, sitting up late at night. Many a time have I gone[Pg 53] out at eleven o'clock at night and wiped my eyes with the dew of the grass in an endeavour to keep myself awake. I managed to get through all these books during the winter and became a convert to the principles contained therein, and thus became an advanced thinker on political and social questions. I think Henry George's books did more to mould my thought on social questions than those of any other writer. About this time I also purchased Adam Smith's Wealth of Nations and Thorold Roger's Six Centuries of Work and Labour. These I soon mastered in all their details. I was thus enabled to take a very broad view on all matters pertaining to Labour and was able to see more clearly the cause of all the gross injustice that was inflicted on my class. I became convinced that if there was a revival in the Labour movement amongst the rural workers, the leaders would have to lift the men's thoughts above the question of the mere raising of wages and would have to take political action and seek to remove the great hindrance to man's progress. I made one mistake. I thought and was convinced that the Liberal Party would do these things, and I was strengthened in my belief by a speech made by the late Mr. Joseph Chamberlain about "ransoming the land back to the people." In my political innocence I thought all politicians were sincere. I was, however, to live to see my faith in some people shattered.

During this year I received again one or two offers to go on a lecturing tour, all of which I declined. I was not, however, to remain in the shade and inactive long. The men again began to be restless and were anxious to have another try at organizing.

[Pg 54]

CHAPTER V

DARE TO BE A UNION MAN

IN the autumn of 1889 the men in Norfolk began to want to form a Union again. This time they appealed to me to lead them in the district in which I lived. For some weeks I refused to take any leading part, but was willing to join a Union. I had only just got settled down comfortably after my terrible eighteen months of bitter persecution, and was just anxious to remain quietly at work. I had no wish to enter into the turmoil of public life. But at last, through the men's constant pleadings, I yielded to the pressure. On November 5, 1889, eleven men formed a deputation and came to my house and stated they represented a large number of men in the district who had decided to form a Union and they wanted me to lead them. I questioned them in order to ascertain if they had seriously thought the matter over. They assured me they had. I also informed them that in my judgment no Union would stand which had no other object than merely to raise wages and that they must go in for something higher than that. I then asked them what Union they wished to form, or did they wish to link up with Arch's Union which was almost defunct. They expressed a wish to form a Union on the same lines as Mr. Rix had formed his, and I was asked to write to Mr. Rix to come over and address one or two meetings and explain the rules of his Union. This I did. Mr. Rix agreed to come, and two meetings were arranged to be held within a fortnight, one at the White Horse Inn[Pg 55] at Cromer and the other at the Free Methodist Church at Aylmerton. Both meetings were packed and were addressed by George Rix and myself. Large numbers gave in their names for membership. It was decided to form a Union on the principle of the rules as explained by Mr. Rix, to be called the Federal Union, Cromer District. The objects of the Union were to be as follows: To improve the social and moral well-being of its members; to assist them to secure allotments and representation on local authorities and even in the Imperial Parliament; to assist members to migrate and emigrate. Ten shillings per week to be paid in strike and victimization pay. Legal advice to be given. Each member to pay 1s. per year harvest levy to enable a member to have his harvest money made up to him in case of a dispute. Each member to pay a contribution of 2¼d. per week, or 9d. per month, 8d. per month to be sent to the district and 1d. per month to be kept by the branch for branch management.

I was elected District Secretary, with no salary fixed for the office. I set about the work in all earnestness, addressing five meetings a week, and writing articles in the weekly papers each week. I kept at my daily work all this time, my employer, Mr. Ketton, putting nothing in my way, allowing me to leave my work an hour early whenever I required to do so and always allowing me to go "one journey." I opened branches at Gresham and Alby Hill (the very place at which I was turned out of my house only five years before). Branches were also opened at Aylsham, Hindolveston, Foulsham, Reepham, Guestwick, Kelling, Southrepps, Gunthorpe, Barney, Guist, Cawston, Bintry, and Lenwade. To many of these places I had to walk, as there was no train service except in a few instances and then only one way. Numbers of the villages were ten and twelve miles from my home. I often left a meeting at ten o'clock at night and reached home at two o'clock in the morning. I[Pg 56] could not cycle in those days. This work continued for over nine months, and during this time I enrolled over 1,000 members at no expense to the Union.

In the autumn of 1890 a general meeting of the members was called, and this meeting decided I should become a whole-time officer and offered me £1 a week. This I at once declined on the ground that the labourers were only receiving 10s. per week, and said I should only take 15s. per week until the labourers received an increase in their wages. From this date, greatly against my wishes, I became a paid official of the Union. Although at this time there was a great revival of the Union spirit, and men were anxious to join a Union, the National Union, of which Mr. Arch was the leader, never again took any hold outside Norfolk. County Unions rose rapidly in other counties under various leaders, Warwickshire under the leadership of Mr. Ben Ryler, Wiltshire was financed by Mr. Louis Anstie of Devizes, and Berkshire was financed by the Misses Skirrett of Reading and led by Mr. T. Quelch. All these were, however, short-lived. In Norfolk we made rapid progress. Arch revived many of his branches in North-west and East Norfolk and progress was made by me in North Norfolk. I helped to start a district in South Norfolk, of which Mr. Edward James of Ditchingham became secretary. My district, not being satisfied with its isolated position, made an offer to the two other districts, namely, East Dereham and Harleston, to become amalgamated in some way, and thus enable us to become a strong force. Both, for reasons best known to themselves, preferred to remain independent. I, however, was convinced that we should never be a force strong enough to meet the farmers, who were rapidly organizing, so long as we remained little isolated Unions. In fact, we were nothing more than tiny rural Unions. I felt rather than continue along those lines I would give the whole thing up, and I placed my views before my district committee—a splendid body[Pg 57] of men. They at once gave me full power to open correspondence with the secretary of a Norwich Union, Mr. Joseph Foyster, now a member of the Norwich bench of magistrates, and the late Mr. Edward Burgess, of "Daylight" fame, who was president of the Union, which was started about the time our Cromer district came into being. A conference of the two Unions was held at the Boar's Head, Surrey Street, Norwich, and after some discussion an agreement to amalgamate was arrived at, each district to hold its own funds and to pay a quarterly levy of 2d. per member to a central fund, which was to be used as a reserve fund in case of a dispute in either district. An Executive was elected which was to have control of the Union. Mr. Edward Burgess was elected president and Messrs. John Leeder, Robert Gotts, J. Spalding, Frank Howes, Joseph Foyster and A. Day were appointed as the Executive. A Mr. Millar of Norwich was elected General Secretary with myself as General Treasurer. I left my position as secretary to the Cromer district. This arrangement did not last long. Mr. Millar soon left the city and was never known to come back again. I was asked to accept the position of General Secretary, which I did. In the Cromer district the following were amongst my most staunch supporters: Messrs. John Leeder, James Leeder, Robert Gotts, Miles Leeder, Edward Holsey, John Spalding, Thomas Painter and Robert Leeder. These men stood by me until the last, never faltering.

The amalgamation being effected and the rules drawn up and registered, we made rapid progress. The Norwich district boundaries were fixed east and south of Norwich. I opened branches at Newton Flotman, Surlingham, Crostwick, Costessey, Eaton, Lakenham, Great Plumstead, Kirby Bedon, Rockland St. Mary, Stoke Holy Cross, Rackheath, and Salhouse. In the two districts in twelve months we reached 3,000 members. Arch's Union also[Pg 58] made progress. The late Mr. Z. Walker was his Norfolk organizer, and that Union reached about 5,000. We never exceeded these figures. Although there was a spirit of rivalry between us, the utmost good feeling prevailed. We never went into each other's district, and always aimed at preventing overlapping, frequently appearing on each other's platforms.

Although I started out with the idea of avoiding strikes, we had not gone far before we found that was impossible. The first struggle we had was at Hindolveston. A Mr. Aberdeen set his men to cut some meadow grass and for this he offered them 3s. 6d. per acre. These terms the men rejected and a lock-out took place. I was informed and I sought an interview with the employer. This was scornfully refused and a message was sent out to me that if I went on to his place again he would set the dog on to me. I indignantly replied that I expected I was dealing with a gentleman, but regretted to find I was dealing with a man who was not sufficiently intelligent to treat another with respect. I also told him I was sure that in less than a week he would send for me and that I would then mete him out the respect he should have shown me. This was what did happen. The men would not consent to see him, but referred him to me. Within a week he sent for me and I settled the dispute by making arrangements for the men to receive 5s. per acre. That was my first effort as a leader and peace-maker. While the dispute lasted the men received the lock-out pay of 10s. per week. The next dispute was at Great Plumstead in the Norwich district and was of a more serious character for one hundred men came out in a demand for 1s. increase in wages. The greatest enthusiasm prevailed, but we found we were in for a very stiff fight. The Farmers' Federation found up a few men to fill the places of those on strike, but we were not dismayed. Enthusiastic meetings were held in every village covered by the Union, and at these songs written by members of Arch's Union[Pg 59] were used by permission of those concerned. These were sung to well-known Sankey hymn tunes.

One favourite song sung to the tune of "Dare to be a Daniel" was:—

Standing by a purpose true,
Heeding your command,
Honour them, the faithful men,
All hail to the Union band.
Chorus.
Dare to be a Union man,
Dare to stand alone.
Dare to have a purpose firm,
Dare to make it known.
Another song we sung was "The Farmer's Boy":—

The sun went down beyond the hills,
Across yon dreary moor.
Weary and lame, a boy there came
Up to a farmer's door.
"Will you tell me if any there be
That will give me employ,
To plough and sow, to reap and mow,
And be a farmer's boy?"
Another was "The Labourer's Anthem."

The sons of Labour in the land
Are rising in their might.
In every town they nobly stand,

And battle for the right.
For long they have been trampled on
By money-making elves,
But the time is come for everyone
To rise and help themselves.
Chorus.
So now, you men, remember then,
This is to be your plan.
Nine hours a day and better pay.
For every working man.
[Pg 60]

This last song reveals that over forty years ago the men had the ideal of a fuller life. The struggle in question lasted nearly a month, but we gained the 1s. increase.

The next battle was fought side by side with Arch's Union. This was over the resistance of a wage reduction. It was on a large scale and was fought with great bitterness. Many of the men were evicted from their homes. This time we were not successful by reason of the fact that the years of 1891 and 1892 were years of great agricultural depression and there were large numbers of unemployed in the villages. After a bitter struggle the men went back to work at the wage offered them. This greatly dispirited the men, though I did my best to encourage them both on the platform and in the press.

[Pg 61]

CHAPTER VI
A DEFEAT AND A VICTORY

In 1892 I fought my first political battle, and for the first time my faith in the Liberal Party received a shock. In this year took place the second General County Council Election, and, by special request of the working men in the Cromer district, I allowed myself to be nominated as a Liberal-Labour candidate for that division, expecting, of course, that I should have the united support of the Liberal Party in whose interests I had worked so hard for several years. Believing them when they said they were anxious that the working man should be represented on all Authorities, one can understand my surprise and astonishment when I found the leading Liberal in the district nominating as my opponent the leading Tory in the district! I lost faith in their sincerity. It was evident they were not prepared to assist the working men to take their share in the government of the country. The contest was turned at once into a class contest. Many of the leading Liberals, as well as the Tories, expressed their disgust at a working man having the audacity to fight for a seat on the Norfolk County Council against a local landlord. My opponent was the late Mr. B. Bond Cabbell, who was returned unopposed at the first election of the Council.

The contest caused the greatest excitement. The late Mr. Henry Broadhurst, M.P., came to my help. The division comprised the towns of Cromer and Sheringham and the following villages: East and West Runton,[Pg 62] Weybourne, Beeston Regis, East and West Beckham, Gresham, Bessingham, Sustead, Aylmerton, Metton and Felbrigg. The contest lasted three weeks, and I covered the whole district and held meetings in every village. All this I did on foot, as I could not cycle and I could not afford to hire a conveyance. The meetings were well attended, and the only help I received was from Mr. Broadhurst and from a few of my own members who were local preachers. The supporters of my opponent manifested the greatest bitterness during the contest, especially the Liberals. So far did they carry this spirit that they descended to publishing a most disgraceful cartoon, depicting a coffin with me lying in it and Broadhurst standing by the side and weeping over me. Underneath were the words: "Puzzle, find Edwards after the election." My opponent strongly condemned such action and threatened to retire unless they withdrew the thing.

The saddest thing of all was that it was my opponent who was dead within three months from the day of the election.

Throughout the election I was booed at by my opponent's supporters, bags of flour and soot were thrown at me, but my supporters heartened me with their cheers. The poll was a heavy one and the votes were counted at Cromer Town Hall on the night of the poll, the result being:—

Bond Cabbell   505
Edwards   455
———
  Majority 50

There was a great crowd gathered outside the hall, my opponents being certain of victory, which they had made every preparation to celebrate. A brass band was there in readiness, and a torchlight procession was formed. I was informed the next morning that the band was worked up to such a state of excitement that the drummer broke[Pg 63] in the end of his drum, which caused much amusement and comment not altogether to the credit of the performers.

The result, however, did not give much satisfaction to the aristocratic party; in fact, they were more bitter than ever. For a working man to run the gentlemen's party so close was more than they could tolerate, for they were afraid that at the next trial of strength Labour might win. Owing to Mr. Bond Cabbell's death another election had to take place, but I decided not to contest the seat again so soon, and my late employer, Mr. R. W. Ketton, came forward and was returned unopposed.

I then turned my attention to perfecting my organization. In the autumn of that year I opened some strong branches at Shipdham, East and West Bradenham, Saham Toney, Ashill, Earlham, Barford, Grimston, Wood Dalling, Swanton Abbott, Hockering and Weston. We were soon doomed to more trouble. Early in 1893 the men got restless. The employers seemed determined to reduce wages further. Arch's Union was seriously involved. Strikes took place at Calthorpe, Erpingham, Southrepps, Northrepps and Roughton, and our Union became involved, as we had members on the farms. Our members also came out at North Barningham, Aylmerton and Alby. A great deal of hard work and anxiety devolved upon me, as I was the only paid official in the Union. Mr. Z. Walker, the only organizer the National Union had at this time, was hardly pressed, as both Unions had members on most of the farms affected, and we frequently met and held joint meetings. I also met Mr. Arch and addressed many meetings with him and we became great friends from that time. We both saw that to have two Unions with the same objects and catering for the same class was a source of weakness, but how to find a way out of it neither of us could see.

We decided, however, so long as the movement lasted, we would work side by side without any friction.

[Pg 64]

The dispute lasted many weeks. The greatest use was made by the employers of the weapon of the tied cottage and many evictions took place.

The magistrates never hesitated when the opportunity presented to grant an eviction order.

In 1893 the Government appointed a Royal Commission to inquire into the administration of the Poor Law. Amongst those appointed to serve on the Commission were the late King (then Prince of Wales), the late Lord Aberdare, Rt. Hon. Joseph Chamberlain, M.P., Henry Broadhurst, M.P., Joseph Arch, M.P. and others. I was invited to give evidence before the Commission upon the following points: Relief in kind; its quality; the amount of allowance; the question of compelling children to support their aged parents. I obtained my facts and prepared my evidence and was called up to London to give it in March 1893. To prove the poorness of the quality of flour allowed by Boards of Guardians I obtained some of this flour and I also bought some of the best flour sold on the market. Needless to say, the contrast was enormous. The members of the Commission were astonished beyond degree at the poorness of the quality of the flour doled out by the Guardians, and I was requested by the Commission to go back and ask my wife to make some bread from the two classes of flour before completing my evidence. This I did, and the following week I took the bread with me before the Commission. The contrast in the bread was more marked even than in the flour. The late King expressed himself as shocked that such stuff was served out to the poor to eat and thanked me for the trouble I had taken in the matter.

Dealing with the inadequacy of the relief, I was requested to give cases of hardship that had come under my personal notice. I presented several cases. One came from the parish of Aylmerton, being that of a widow left with four little children, one a baby in arms. She was allowed 6d. per week each for three children[Pg 65] and nothing for the fourth; half a stone of flour each for three and nothing for herself. In those days a widow was supposed to keep herself and one child. This poor widow's suffering was beyond degree, but this was only a sample of the suffering and extreme poverty of those who had lost the breadwinner. The case of the aged poor was even worse. I presented cases, giving the names of aged couples living together and only receiving one stone of flour and 2s. 6d. in money, and of widows (aged) receiving only half a stone of flour and 1s. 6d. in money. In fact, my own mother was only allowed 2s. 6d. per week and no flour and, further, I was called upon by the Aylsham Board of Guardians to contribute 1s. 3d. per week towards the sum allowed her by the Board, although I was only receiving 15s. per week with which to keep myself and my wife.

I also named several cases of extreme hardship of children being called upon to support their parents. I gave the cases of two agricultural labourers named Hazelwood, living at Baconsthorpe. Both were married men with large families, one, I believe, had eight children. They were both summoned before the Cromer magistrates by the Erpingham Board of Guardians to show cause why they should not contribute towards the maintenance of their aged parents.

I was cross-examined on my evidence for some hours by Mr. Joseph Chamberlain. At the close of my examination I was thanked by the late King and the other members of the Commission for my evidence. The Commission held their sittings in the Queen's Robing Room in the House of Lords. When my evidence was published it caused quite a sensation in the country, and I think the report of this Commission hastened on the passing of the District and Parish Councils Act. About this time I grew so disgusted with the treatment meted out to my mother that I absolutely refused to contribute any more towards the sum granted her by them. I told[Pg 66] the Board they could stop the miserable 2s. 6d. per week and this they did forthwith. My wife and I at once gave notice to the landlord of the cottage in which my mother had lived for fifty years, the rent of which we had paid between us, and I decided to take her to our home and look after her. My sister had the furniture with the exception of the bed on which my mother slept and an old chest of drawers. I kept my mother until she died on February 5, 1892, without receiving a penny from anyone.

In 1894 the Government brought in a Bill known as the District and Parish Councils Bill, which provided for the establishment of a Council in every parish having a population of 300 and over, and the placing of the obtaining of allotments for the working classes in the hands of the Council, together with the appointing of trustees for Parish Charities. It also sought to abolish all property qualification in election as Guardians. Mr. Z. Walker and I jointly entered into a campaign during the passage of the Bill through Parliament, Mr. Arch paying as many visits to the county as his parliamentary duties would permit. We also had the valuable assistance of the English Land Restoration League, as it was then called, Mr. Frederick Verinder being the General Secretary. The League sent down one of their vans and a lecturer.

The Trades Union Congress was held in Norwich this year (1894). I attended the Congress as delegate from the Norfolk and Norwich Amalgamated Labour League and moved a resolution on the tied cottage system.

At the end of the session the Bill became law, and by the instructions of my Executive I set about preparing to put the Act in force. I held meetings in every village where we had branches of the Union and explained the provisions of the Act. By the time the first meetings were held to elect the Parish Councils in many of our villages we had got our men ready and well posted up[Pg 67] in the mode of procedure as to nominations and how to carry on.

The first meeting was held in December in the village in which I lived. We held a preliminary meeting in the schools to explain the Act. This meeting was attended by the Rev. W. W. Mills, the Rector of the parish, who caused some little amusement by his constant personal interjections. For some years for some reason he had shown a personal dislike to me, and he never lost an opportunity to manifest this spirit of dislike. What influenced him I never could understand, but he always seemed jealous of my influence in the village as a Nonconformist. A few days after this meeting was held the Rector came to my house to inform me that Mrs. Mills was being nominated as a candidate for the District Council, and I informed him that I was also being nominated. He expressed a wish that the contest might be friendly. I informed him that so far as I was concerned it would. He then accused me of being the cause of the meeting referred to above being disorderly, which I stoutly denied. He then called me a liar, and it looked for a few moments as if we were in for a scuffle, for I threatened to put him out of my house and began to take steps to do so. He at once rose from his seat and rushed to the door before I could lay hands on him, but in getting away he caught my hand in the door and knocked the skin off my knuckles. My wife was in the next room, and had she not appeared on the scene I do not know what would have happened. She got between us, took the Rector by the collar and put him out of the yard. This event caused some little excitement in the village.

At the meeting held for the election of Parish Councillors all the Labour members nominated were elected. We had nominated sufficient candidates to fill all the seats but one, and this was taken by Mr. Groom, the schoolmaster. The parish of Felbrigg was also joined to Aylmerton for the purpose of forming the Parish Council,[Pg 68] and it became known as the Aylmerton-cum-Felbrigg Parish Council. At the first meeting of the Council I was elected chairman. I was also elected on the Beckham Parish Council on which I served for some years, and I was also one of the charity trustees. One of the first things we did on the Aylmerton Council was to obtain allotments for the labourers in the parishes of Aylmerton and Felbrigg. In fact, our enthusiasm to do something was so great that it was the cause of our undoing, for at the next election we all got defeated, and I took no more interest in the affairs of the parish while I lived there.

At the District Council election I beat my opponent by four votes. My wife was elected for the parish of East and West Beckham unopposed, Mr. Barker was elected for Sustead, Mr. T. Self for Felbrigg, Mr. Walter Towler for Edgefield and Mr. B. Johnson for Sheringham. Thus we started the new Erpingham District Council and Board of Guardians with six direct Labour representatives, which beat the record in all rural England. I was a member of this Council for eighteen years and my wife for ten years.

The reception we received at the first meeting of the Council was rather mixed. Many of the members were rather alarmed at so many Labour members being elected, particularly myself, whom they looked upon as being the leader of the group, and of course I was looked upon as being a rebel, out for revolution, to upset law and order, and to go in for most indiscriminate outdoor relief. Our arrival at the Board was rather late, and on entering the room we found all the other members present discussing the probable events of the day. As soon as I appeared in the room I saw some of the members point to me and remark, that I was "the fellow." Well, it was quite true, we were there for business and to make a great alteration in the administration of the Poor Law. On settling down to work we found the[Pg 69] outdoor relief allowed by this Board was as follows: Aged couples, one stone of flour and 2s. 6d. per week, and in a few special cases 3s. per week; single persons, half a stone of flour and 1s. 6d. per week; young widow with family 6d. per week and half a stone of flour for all the children with the exception of one, which the widow was expected to keep as well as herself. We found another shameful practice in existence. If the late husband of the recipient was in a sick club, the widow was requested to show all her bills as evidence of how she had spent her husband's funeral money before any relief was granted.

This seems almost incredible, but it is true. We made an early attempt to alter this scandalous state of things, as the following account of a debate that took place will prove. Although we did not get the improvements we aimed at, still we made some advancement, and it encouraged us to aim very soon at other improvements. We Labour members made strict inquiries into the conditions of the poor. We also found in those days that the Relieving Officers had not advanced far from their predecessors in the treatment of the poor and would take any excuse to deprive the poor of relief. On going to the Board meeting one day my wife found that a poor sick and aged widow had had her relief stopped by the Relieving Officer, the excuse being that the woman had given birth to an illegitimate child. This the officer said he knew to be true as the woman had told him so. This astounded my wife, as she knew it was impossible for such a thing to have happened, and she undertook to investigate the matter. This she did, and was able to inform the Board that the so-called illegitimate child was thirty years of age, married, and a mother herself. Needless to say, we Labour members did not fail to denounce this cruel act for all we were worth and we got the poor woman her money put on again. The Relieving Officer was made to pay her her back money himself and never to come to the Board again with such a story.

[Pg 70]

The next question we tackled was the relief given in kind. We found that meat tickets ordered by the doctor had been refused in numbers of cases, so much so that the doctors had begun to complain. I raised the question on the Board and I found up a clause in the Poor Law Act that prohibited the Guardians from refusing to give relief in kind ordered by the doctor. It caused a good deal of discussion, but we got the matter put right. The quality of the flour allowed to the poor next came under our notice. One week a poor widow living in my village brought me a loaf of bread she had made from the flour the Relieving Officer had left her that week. One could take the middle out and leave the crust standing like two walls. My wife gave the woman some of her own flour, took the other flour and made it into bread herself, with the same result. I took this bread, with a loaf my wife made from her own flour, to the meeting of the Guardians, and strange to say the Rev. Casson, living at Mundesley, fourteen miles from where I lived, also took some. We denounced this treatment and all kinds of excuses were forthcoming. During the discussion it came to light that the contractor was only a journeyman, and that he took the contract for his master. The result of this exposure was the stopping of all relief in kind so far as flour was concerned. The following report of the debate appeared in the Eastern Weekly Leader:—

The Rev. Casson brought up some bread and flour from Mundesley, and Mr. Edwards brought two loaves of bread and three samples of flour from Aylmerton, and they were laid on the table for the Guardians to inspect. The bread had a very bad appearance. The Rev. Casson moved that the contractor who supplied this flour to the poor in the Southrepps district be named, and that early steps be taken to bring him to punishment, and that his name be for ever struck out from the list of contractors of this Union. The rev. gentleman said that the man who could be villain enough to supply the poor with such stuff as this called flour deserved to be punished to the utmost limit of the law. (Cries of "Prove the flour is bad.") The Rev. Casson: "I have[Pg 71] brought a sample of the bread and flour here, and I will ask any Guardian if he thinks it is fit for human food, and are we as Guardians going to sit quietly by and see our poor served with such stuff as this? It is not fit for the beasts to eat." At this stage the rev. gentleman grew very excited, and was exhibiting his sample of bread and flour, when Mr. Richard Mack, a co-opted member, took the bread and put it into the fire. The rev. gentleman then moved excitedly that Mr. Mack be named and expelled for the day for his dastardly and cowardly act—(great disorder).—Mr. Mack, he continued, had destroyed the only protection these poor people had.—Mr. Edwards said he rose as a protest against the conduct of Mr. Mack. He had been brought into contact with a large number of people, and he must say he never saw a more ungentlemanly act in his life. He was surprised that any gentleman should so forget himself as to treat another gentleman as Mr. Mack had treated the Rev. Casson when he was advocating the rights of the poor. (Cries of "shame.") Mr. Edwards: "It is a shame, and I appeal to the Chairman to protect the Rev. Casson and obtain for him a fair hearing." (Loud applause.) Mr. Edwards added, "Let anyone dare to destroy my sample of bread and I will soon show them what course I will take."—Mr. Towler said he thought it was most unfair that the Rev. Casson should be interrupted. Surely gentlemen were not afraid these things should be brought to light.—The Rev. Casson said he felt it very much that Mr. Mack should throw his bread into the fire, as it was the protection these poor people had whose cause he was advocating. Speaking on the flour, he said the complaint did not come from one person only, nor yet from one village, for the same complaint came from Trimingham, and his friend Mr. Edwards had brought the same complaint from Aylmerton, miles away from Mundesley, and he hoped the Guardians would bring the man to punishment that had been guilty.—Mr. Edwards said it was with mixed feelings that he seconded the Rev. Casson's resolution. He was pleased that he was on the Board to watch the interest of the poor, and he was pleased that the Rev. Casson had spoken out as he had. He could assure the Rev. Casson that he would receive the warm gratitude of hundreds of poor people for the course he had taken. At the same time he very much regretted that any man could be found in this country calling itself Christian so cruel as to act as this contractor had done. He, Mr. Edwards, had been very careful to bring flour as well as bread, and he had also got bread and flour from different persons so that it could not be said that it was all of one make and was the fault of the maker.—Mr. Waters moved as an amendment that we have some of the flour taken from the other sacks and sent to two or three bakers to test it before naming the[Pg 72] contractor. Mr. Waters said he did not wish it to go forth that he did not wish the poor people to have good flour, but he thought they ought to be sure first that the flour was bad, or the Board might find themselves sued for libel. In his opinion the bread produced was baked badly and the yeast was not good.—Mr. Daplyn seconded the amendment.—Mrs. Edwards said Mr. Waters had no right to speak of the bread in the way he had. The bread which her husband had brought from Aylmerton was made of the same yeast hers was made from, and hers was very good—good enough even for Mr. Waters to eat if he wished; and further, she knew the woman that made the bread, and she could assure the Guardians she was a good bread-maker. She was sure it was not the fault of the maker nor yet of the yeast, but of the flour; and she would challenge anyone that had any knowledge of flour to prove that the flour produced was good. She could assure the Guardians that her neighbours and sister working-woman could make as good bread as anyone else if they had the flour to make it with.—Mr. Broadhurst said he hoped the Rev. Casson would not press his vote of censure upon Mr. Mack, for he thought he had no ill feeling.—Mr. Mack apologised and said he only put the bread into the fire through fun. He was anxious the poor should have good flour.—Mr. Broadhurst, continuing, said any contractor or contractors who could be found to conspire together to supply the poor people with such stuff as this called bread ought to be brought to book. He would ask anyone if they thought such stuff as this was fit for human food? Why, he would not give it to his dog, much less offer it to a poor human being. The poor ask for bread and we give them stuff fit only to make paste with.—Mr. Waters: "We do not supply them with bread, but with flour."—Mr. Broadhurst: "Oh, very well. Flour, if you like to call it such. I do not. But we have it here on the evidence of one of the ladies that some of the bread is made with the very same yeast that her bread is made with, and hers is good; and further that she knows one of the women who made the bread, and that she knows her to be a good bread-maker. Why should they doubt this Guardian's words? Further, we have bread and flour brought from villages miles apart, and it would be impossible for them to conspire together for the purpose of trumping up a complaint. This affair to-day is another strong argument in favour of giving the poor money instead of relief in kind, and all honour to those gentlemen who have brought this matter before the Board; they will receive the thanks of thousands of people when they read the debate."—Mr. Kimm, the Relieving Officer, said the sub-contractor had offered to take the other sacks back.—Mr. Broadhurst: "Subcontractor! What, do you mean to say that this Board allows its business to be done in this fashion? Do you mean to say that[Pg 73] this Board puts out contracts and then allows the contractor to sub-contract? There is no wonder then that the poor people are supplied with such stuff as this. Why, if this kind of proceeding is allowed to continue, this Board will become the laughing-stock of all the country, and further, who are we to put our hands on if this thing be proved? I would like to ask the Clerk who the contractor is?"—The Clerk: "Mr. Tuck of Hempstead."—Mr. Daplyn: "Why, he is only a journeyman miller and works for Mr. Bird."—Mr. Edwards: "Yes, and he is sweated by someone else; that is how this Board does its business."—Mr. Broadhurst, continuing, said this was a strange revelation, and he was astonished that business men on the Board should allow this kind of thing to exist. Here is a working man made a tool for someone else to sweat, and then he puts it out to sub-contract to someone else, and this someone else sweats someone else. What ever had the House Committee been doing?—The Rev. Fitch rose to a point of order; the Committee were not to blame, as the recommendation of the Committee was accepted by the whole Board. He was a member of the Committee and never knew before now that Tuck was a working man.—Mr. Edwards said he had just found it out, and he thought the Committee ought to have found it out before.—Mr. Waters said the Committee had put out the contract to Tuck for years.—Mr. Broadhurst: "If that is so it is most unsatisfactory."—Continuing, Mr. Broadhurst asked who the sub-contractor was, and the Clerk replied, "Mr. Press."—Mr. Robins Cook: "Yes, and a very respectable tradesman too, and he would not do a wrong act if he knew it."—Mr. Broadhurst: "There is no one has said anything about the respectability of any man, but this sub-contractor has admitted that the flour was bad."—Mr. Waters: "No, no."—Mr. Broadhurst: "Mr. Waters says no, no, but the letter states that he would take the remaining sacks back, and what is that but admitting it?"—Mr. Bugden said that if the mover of the amendment and resolution would consent, he would suggest that a committee be formed to inquire into the matter, and get some of the flour from the remaining sacks and make it up and report to the Board.—Mr. Waters and Mr. Daplyn said they would withdraw their amendment in favour of Mr. Bugden's suggestion.—Rev. Casson said he was not disposed to withdraw his resolution, for it was only an attempt to baulk the question. (Cries of "Order.") The rev. gentlemen said the Committee had set up a dummy to shoot at. (Cries of "No, no.") Rev. Casson: "But you have; you only got us a journeyman miller to deal with."—Mr. Edwards said if Mr. Bugden could assure him there would be no delay and the matter thoroughly gone into, he would be disposed to advise the Rev. Casson to withhold his resolution until this day fortnight.—To[Pg 74] this the Rev. Casson agreed.—Mr. Bugden then moved that a committee of five be appointed to investigate the matter and get some of the flour from the remaining sacks and make up for a test, and that the Relieving Officer go home at once and get the flour and seal it up.—Mr. Waters seconded the resolution, and it was carried that the committee consist of Mr. Waters, Mr. Edwards, Mr. Bone, and Mrs. Johnson. It was further resolved, on the motion of Mr. Edwards, seconded by Mr. Farmer, that the poor in the Southrepps district receive money equivalent to flour for the next fortnight.

[Pg 75]

CHAPTER VII
DARK DAYS

The continuance of bad seasons since 1890, with low prices, had brought about a great depression in agriculture. Thousands of labourers were discharged, and the greatest distress prevailed amongst the rural population. Prices went down to the lowest level. Thousands of coombs of barley were sold at 9s. per coomb and of wheat at 12s. per coomb. Had not the root crop been exceptionally good and feeding stuffs very cheap, which gave them a fair profit on their cattle, many of the farmers must have been ruined. But, as now, the labourer was the first to be called upon to bear the heaviest part of the burden. His wages were reduced to 11s. per week. This greatly dispirited them. They began to leave the Unions in large numbers, and towards the close the Unions had become almost helpless.

The political opponents of the Union saw their opportunity to spread disunity amongst the men. They employed a Mr. A. L. Edwards to start a Union in opposition to the others, and this became known as the Labourers' Independent Federation, which proved to be a free labour organization. The man was employed by the other side. His method of attack was to get the balance sheets of the other Unions. The first Union he attacked was the Suffolk Labourers' Federation, whose General Secretary was Mr. Robinson of Ipswich. Mr. Edwards endeavoured to become a member of this Union, but was rejected. He next attacked Arch in a most unfair[Pg 76] manner. After a while he attacked me unceasingly. Hundreds of thousands of leaflets were printed and scattered broadcast, and these followed me about wherever I went for years. This must have cost the Tory Party hundreds of pounds. It had its effect. The leaflets were headed: "How the Labourers' Money is Spent." The men left the Union, and I soon became convinced that the whole movement was going.

In the early part of 1894 a new weekly paper was started in Norwich known as the Eastern Weekly Leader. The Rev. Charles Peach became its editor. This was started as an advanced Radical paper; in fact, had it been in existence to-day, it would have ranked as a Labour paper. It was, however, like all other advanced papers, doomed to have a short life. I became a local correspondent and agent, and I at once reduced my Union salary to 10s. per week. This, however, did not save the Union from decay.

The columns of this paper were open to every phase of the Labour movement. Stirring articles appeared in the paper week by week aimed at encouraging the labourers. I worked hard to push its sale amongst the labourers and for a few months it went well, but early in 1895 it became evident that it would have to go under.

By the end of 1894 the condition of the people had become considerably worse. Arch and myself had become terribly disheartened. We met to discuss the best thing to do to keep the Unions alive. His sick benefit side had become insolvent. The trade and industrial departments had borrowed money from the sick fund, contrary to rule. Great friction arose between Arch and the trustees of his sick fund, Mr. George Mitchell and Mr. Howard Evans. They locked up the funds, a law suit followed and the two trustees at once resigned. Happily for us we had no sick fund connected with our Union. Arch and myself agreed that we would continue for another year, if we could, and undertook to write[Pg 77] an article in the papers pointing out the conditions and urging upon the labourers the necessity of banding themselves together and, if possible, to attract public sympathy. I wrote as follows to the Weekly Leader:—

The year 1894 has gone and 1895 has had its birth this week. I propose to still further comment upon the condition of the workers for the purpose of throwing further light upon the subject and enlightening the mind of the public upon this most important problem, for it is every day evident that one-half of the world does not know how the other half lives. First let us look at the conditions under which the agricultural labourer works and lives. His work is not only laborious but its very nature must necessarily be unhealthy. He is exposed to the scorching rays of the sun during the summer months, but also exposed to all wets and colds during the winter months. During the summer months in many cases the labourer leaves his home at the early hours in the morning to enable him to reach his work by six in the morning, and very often the first greeting he receives is a surly growl from his employer. He goes to work, and his hours of labour are from five in the morning to five in the afternoon. In the winter his work is from the dawn of daylight to its close. It is only those who have experienced it can possibly have any knowledge of the conditions under which the agricultural labourer works and the suffering and privations he has to undergo in performing his daily task. It is quite fresh to the mind of the writer of these comments when he had to shelter beneath a hedgerow to be screened from the piercing winds, and his teeth have chattered in his head, and many a time has he been soaked through with wet.

The labourer's home after his day's work is done, if a home it can be called, is of the worst kind. Although, through the industry of the wife, it is a great deal more comfortable than one might expect, considering the scanty income and the wretched condition of the cottages in which they have to live. Very often during the winter months the first thing that has to be done after his return home is to strip himself of his wet clothes, and the wife has to place them in front of the small fire to dry them fit for the morning, and the small room is made damp. The houses in which the labourer has to live are neither sanitary, water-tight, nor wind-tight. In a house where I was staying a few days ago the poor people informed me that only a few nights previous they found themselves suddenly awakened by their bedclothes being soaked by the water that was coming through the roof. Can it be wondered at, then, that sickness is so prevalent amongst the workers? This description is no idle fable. In many cases the labourer[Pg 78] barely ever sees his children by daylight, except on Sunday. But even those cottages, in spite of their wretched condition, the labourer has to hire under such conditions as cannot fail to place him in a position of the most abject slavery, and cause his wages to come down to the lowest minimum, stunt his intellect, and affect his morals. Under the present social system the labourer feels compelled to look upon the man who employs him as a benefactor, and also to feel himself under some obligation to him. The unscrupulous employer is quick to see this, and soon looks upon it as the natural order of things that it should be so, and that he is quite right in treating his men in this manner, and in paying them just what wage he pleases, without thought or care whether they are able to keep body and soul together.

There have been so many men running about our county endeavouring to impress upon the minds of the working classes that Trade Unions are of no benefit, except to keep a few men with a living, that I am prompted to say a word or two. This idea has taken hold of a number of men, and thousands of labourers in Norfolk have become indifferent about the matter during the past year, whilst those who have been the means of upsetting them with their Free Labour Federation have made no attempt to improve the position of the labourers of this county. Everyone sees now that these parties are kept by political agents, and their only object is to get the labourers divided so that they may get a political advantage at the next General Election. The reason I speak out so plainly is this: If you watch the papers you will find that the men imported into this county during the past twelve months to upset Trades' Unions are generally employed at bye-elections. The Brigg election is a witness to this assertion. We have no cause to be ashamed of the history of Trades' Unions; their object was to demand a living wage for work performed, and also for gaining social and political reforms all along the line. Have we succeeded? I contend we have, and have done more for the improvement of the working classes than all the blackleg crew from Suffolk or any other county. We may not have succeeded in every fight that we have been engaged in, but the reason for it has been because the men have not been united. Look at the miners' struggle last year, it was most severe, and showed to the country the power of combination and endurance on the part of the sons of toil. Have not these men benefited by their Union? I contend that they have, and the same benefits might be derived if all the labourers were united in this country. Their object would not be to crush the farmer, but to have a standard wage, which should be a living wage, and not subject to alterations two or three times in the year. By their combination they could enforce this, and it would be more satisfactory to all parties [Pg 79]concerned. Moreover, we should have less petty little strikes which accomplish nothing. It is only by combination that you can demand a living wage, and I contend the present advantages which the men enjoy are mainly due to the work of the Union in the past. We not only went in for the wage question, but also for political power, and to-day we enjoy it. The labourers have the vote and can put whom they choose into Parliament to represent them, and they have had pluck enough in this county to put a labourer into Parliament to represent one of the divisions, and I may say he represents the whole county of agricultural labourers, and is ready to serve them in that house at any time when their questions come up.

Unemployment amongst the labourers increased. The Government of the day appointed a Royal Commission to inquire into the cause of the depression in agriculture and sent inspectors into the various counties to hold inquiries. Mr. (now Sir) Henry Rew was sent down to Norfolk, and I attended before him and gave evidence, upon which he commented in giving his report. Nothing, however, came out of the Commission's report. The fact was it was too big a question for the Tory Government to tackle. During the winter I attended several meetings and gave advice. I told the men if the employers would not employ them they were not to starve, but to throw themselves and their families upon the rates. Many of them did. On my own Board I moved a resolution to put into force an old Act of Parliament that enabled the Guardians to hire fifty acres of land on which to set the unemployed to work and to pay the men labourers' wages. This, of course, was defeated, but I warned the Board that the day was not far distant when they or some other authority would have to deal with the problems of the land and the unemployed, for the men would not starve. On May 26th the following article by me appeared in one of the Norfolk papers, showing the acute stage the question had reached:—

My friend Mr. Z. Walker, commenting on the labour question in one of the Norfolk papers, made a statement in reference to the[Pg 80] above question which if true—and my experience will re-echo the same thing—will cast a stigma upon our boasted civilization. Mr. Walker stated that he knew of cases in Norfolk of young men who are in the Union workhouse for no other cause than that the farmers will not employ them, and that other men are quite willing to work, but find it hard to obtain employment. Now, the question that presents itself to one's mind is: Is it right for men to starve and remain idle while the land is thirsting for labour? And I should say every right-thinking man will answer "No," emphatically "No"; and those young men named by Mr. Walker took the wisest course—far better than migrating to the large towns, to unduly compete with their fellow workmen. Nevertheless, it is a disgrace to the age in which we live that men should be found willing and anxious for work, but unable to find it.

This question of the unemployed is daily taking a more serious aspect. Year by year this menacing army of unemployed is on the increase, not only in this country, but in every other country, go where you may, and whatever form of Government it is, democratic or autocratic. Even in America, where everyone has equal political rights, and where we are told the Presidential chair is open to any man who has the ability and tact to work himself up to it, however humble his parentage may be, the question of the unemployed is becoming so serious that men stand and look on with amazement, and the wildest schemes are propagated as a remedy—schemes which if carried out would throw society into disorder and confusion.

Various have been the reasons given for the existing state of things. In England we are told it is our fiscal policy, known as Free Trade, while others say it is our monetary system. In America, a highly protected country, reformers say it is Protection and advocate Free Trade. The same thing exists in all the nations in Europe. With this state of affairs, small wonder that some men are beginning to think that it matters not what form of Government we have. Various reforms have been passed in recent years which have been beneficial in themselves, but they do not seem to have touched the fringe of the question; still the bitter cry of poverty is heard from the workless ones, and still we are horrified by the fact that men and women are driven to despair and to take their own lives, while others are urged to commit most dastardly acts. The Local Government Act will do something to alter the present evils if the workers take proper interest in it and put men on the District Councils who are in touch with them, and it will go a long way towards establishing the right of the people to use the earth.

But we must have something far more drastic than that: we must go to the root of the matter; everyone who has the true[Pg 81] interest of the country and the cause of humanity at heart must set himself to work to find out the cause of the evil, and when once this is done must approach the question with an unselfish spirit, and however drastic the reform may be that is necessary it will have to be done. I confess that I hold more advanced views on the land and other social questions than some of the Labour leaders, but that is brought about after having watched every movement that has been set on foot for the abolition of human suffering and carefully studying the various arguments used in advocating various schemes to deal with social problems and the various causes assigned for the present state of things.

I am satisfied that nothing will ever prove effectual but the abolition of our present land system. This huge monopoly has, like Belshazzar, been weighed in the balance and found wanting. All history condemns the idea that a few people have absolute right to the use of the earth, to the exclusion of the rest. History informs us that landowners were simply trustees to the State for the land held, and were under the obligation to provide and equip at their own cost the defences of the nation, besides having other onerous dues to pay and duties to perform. But gradually the landholders, who are now called landlords, after having seized all public and Church property they could lay their hands upon, shifted these burdens from their own shoulders on to those of the people. The existing land system places the landlords in the position of antagonists of the general public, and the people are thrown into the grasp of a huge octopus, which is dragging them down to despair and the workers to the depths of misery, crippling the trade and commerce of the world.

This landed system, which has grown up under successive Kings and Governments, and is now upheld by bad laws, is a crime against the people; it is a violation of Divine order and of the inalienable rights of mankind. It has created pauperism, that awful evil which inflicts an injustice and cruelty upon the honest workers and drives one out of every four into the Union workhouse. Farmers are ruined and willing workers are cast off the land they would gladly cultivate to seek a miserable existence in overcrowded cities, where their presence aggravates the miseries already existing. This system is a danger to society, and if not speedily remedied must bring disastrous consequences.

This question of the unemployed and the social well-being of the people is strictly a religious one: When I first entered into public life some of my closest friends with whom I had been in Christian society for several years were astounded when on one occasion I preached a sermon on the Labour movement on the Sunday, and I was severely taken to task for so doing. Some months before, yielding to the wishes of the labourers to champion[Pg 82] their cause, I seriously thought the question over, as I felt that I could not on any account engage in anything that in any way clashed with my Christian principles, and it was because I was convinced that the great disparity existing in the social condition of the people and the gross inequality in the distribution of wealth were contrary to the Divine wish, and that the benevolent intentions of God were not being carried out, that I gave way to the wishes of the labouring men to advocate the cause of the honest toilers. I consider that every time I attend a Labour meeting I attend a religious service in the strictest sense of the word. What movement can be more sacred than the one that has for its object the uplifting of man, the beautifying of human nature, and the restoring of that likeness and image of God which man has so long lost? Poverty is the cause of so much evil and degradation. Poverty is the prolific mother of vice, disease, and all that is vile and ungodlike. Poverty, then, is what we are trying to abolish. What we claim is this, then, that the question of the poverty of the people, brought about by the selfishness of man and the undue haste of the few to get rich at the expense of the many, is a religious question, and it will not be until we get pure homes, sanitary houses, good living, good work, and sufficient to keep every man employed with a good and fair living wage that we shall ever hope to have a healthy and purified state of society; never until all classes truly realize the iniquity of our present social system, and the morality of Christ's Gospel finds a lodgment in our hearts, can we hope to make men think and act as men; never until the religion of humanity enables us to claim succour for the little ones, manhood for ourselves, and justice for the oppressed shall we ever have a happy and pure nation.

In spite of the indifferent attitude of those we represented, my wife and I pressed on with our work on the Board. She was elected to the House Committee, which gave her an opportunity to find out many of the existing abuses in the House. One abuse was the treatment meted out to the poor unfortunate girls whose lot it was to go into the House for confinement. A system of punishment had sprung up in such cases. The Guardians appeared to have come to the conclusion that it was their duty to punish the girls severely, many of whom were more sinned against than sinning. In fact, the Poor Law encouraged them to do so; hence the poor girls were set[Pg 83] to do the hardest work that could be found them. They were often kept at the wash-tub when they were not fit to be there. On one occasion my wife paid a surprise visit to the House and found a poor girl hard at work in the laundry who she thought would have been in the infirmary. The girl said she was there only five days. My wife raised the question at the next meeting of the committee and said some very straight things and protested very strongly. Some of the members said they were surprised that my wife should not be in favour of punishment, for they must put down immorality. My wife retorted that she was not encouraging immorality—in fact she had endeavoured to set her poor sister an example—but she was against cruel treatment being meted out to her poor unfortunate sisters and, unless the practice was stopped, she would raise the whole question at the full Board. This practice was at once stopped, and after that no girl was ever set to work until at least twelve days had elapsed after her confinement. The tramps next came under our notice. We found they were set to work to pick an almost impossible quantity of oakum, and if they failed to pick the allotted quantity, they were kept in the tramp ward for two days. Despite this the Guardians lost money on the business. We raised the whole question and moved that the business should be abolished. The strongest opposition to this being done was raised and at first we were defeated. But we kept at it and finally we got it carried. I also found that the tramps were kept none too warm. One Sunday afternoon I paid a surprise visit to the tramps' ward, and on a cold November evening I found there was no fire in the ward. I denounced this inhuman treatment at the Board. Again the old idea was trotted out. These parasites, living on the community, must be punished. I replied with the stinging retort that the tramps were not the only people born tired, and I moved that in future during the winter months there should be a fire in the[Pg 84] ward. After a good deal of discussion this was carried. The next subject we tackled was the old peoples' dress. We moved that the distinctive dress should be abolished and that the old ladies should be dressed in a more homelike way. This was also adopted, but I don't think the old ladies took to it very kindly. Still it was a step in the right direction. The dietary table was taken in hand, and a great improvement was made in this direction, and month by month we gradually increased the out relief.

An amusing incident happened to me one Sunday when I was conducting a religious service in a little chapel. A poor old widow sat right against the pulpit. Her out relief had been increased from 1s. 6d. to 3s. per week. After I had finished the service the old lady came up to me, put her arms round my neck and, as innocently as a child of two, kissed me and pronounced God's blessing upon me, saying she hoped I would live for ever.

Early in 1896 a Poor Law conference was held at Norwich, and the Board unanimously elected me as one of their representatives. I was put on almost all the committees, for by this time a much better feeling existed on the Board. We began to understand each other and we gave each other credit for honest intentions.

Under the District and Parish Councils Act the Guardians were also deemed to be District Councillors, except those living in urban districts. The Council became the Highways Authority and took over all the parish roads. They also became the Sanitary Authority. I was put on the committees for these purposes and our first fight for Labour commenced. As the Highways Authority, the Council became a large employer of labour, and when we came to fixing the wages and hours a stiff fight commenced. I moved that the men should receive 2s. 6d. per day or 15s. per week. This proposition filled the employers on the Council with alarm, and we were met[Pg 85] with the point that, if we paid that wage, all the labourers would become dissatisfied and would want the same, and they could not afford it. I retorted that it was the duty of the Council to set an example and pay a living wage. This was defeated, but we did manage to get passed that the roadmen received 1s. per week more than the labourers. In the course of two or three years we tackled the housing question, and before I left the Council in 1910 we had adopted Part III of the Housing Act and had built houses at Briston and Edgefield. I look back with more pleasure to the work I was able to do for my class on this Board and Council than to any other work I have done during the whole of my long public life. I had the satisfaction of knowing that comfort and pleasure was brought into many a poor old person's home.

We commenced the year 1895 with a very large decrease of members. Our balance sheet showed our income to be down nearly 50 per cent., and although I had my salary reduced from 18s. to 10s. and the Executive had cut down expenses by one half, our savings were very small. We had several small disputes. The Executive thought they would have one more effort to revive the Union. Again the English Land Restoration League came to our aid and sent another of their vans and a lecturer down free for the summer months. Many villages where branches had fallen through were visited. Thousands of leaflets on land and labour questions were distributed by the League. The Tory and capitalist party worked equally hard the other way. At first they devoted all their energies against Arch and published most scandalous leaflets about his balance sheet that shocked every fair-minded man in all political parties. I was the first to publish the balance sheet of 1894. No sooner had I done this than they attacked me more ferociously than they had done Arch. They manipulated[Pg 86] the sheet in a shameful manner, so much so that even the employers were ashamed of such tactics. It had, however, its desired effect and by the end of 1895 both Unions had actually become defunct. During the year I went without my 10s. per week, knowing the Union would collapse within a few months, and I received my income from the Weekly Leader. On December 7, 1895, I wrote to the Leader the following open letter:—

Fellow Workers,—The year of 1895 is fast slipping beneath our feet, and it becomes us all who are in any way interested in labour to take a retrospect of the past months, and also to take a view of the present condition of the working classes, in order that a correct impression of the condition of the labouring classes during the year 1895 may be obtained. As one of the much despised Labour leaders I feel that the time has come when we must speak out plainly to the working men, and show them their exact position. Now, first I wish to point out to you that so far as combination is concerned, and the means to help yourselves to resist unfair treatment, you stand in a far worse condition than you did at the commencement of the year. You were then in a wretchedly disorganized condition—not more than one out of every four of the labourers being in an organization of any kind—but to-day you are in a far worse state of disorganization, and you are altogether powerless to help yourselves in any way; and what is far worse, there has been growing up amongst you a spirit of distrust and prejudice, until to-day your ranks are all chaos and confusion. You seem to be like Ishmaelites, every man's hand turned against the other. I must confess that I for one did expect better things of you. With the District and Parish Councils Act just coming into force, I hoped that new life would rise amongst you, and that you would endeavour to make the most of the opportunities that presented themselves to you, and that by this time you would have been in a much better position. But my hopes have been blighted and now I despair of you. All hopes that you as a class will make any effort to lift yourselves from your down-trodden state have vanished. Such being so, many of us are seriously considering whether the time has not come for us to step out of the field and leave you to fight your way the best you can. Now, so far as the actual state of Labour is concerned, your outlook for the future is most gloomy for reasons already stated, and at present the condition of labour is not very much improved. At the commencement of this year your wages[Pg 87] as agricultural labourers were 10s. per week; flour was 11d. and 1s. per stone. At present your wages are 10s. per week, and flour 1s. 2d. and 1s. 3d. per stone, and thus with a family using five stones of flour per week, as hundreds of you do, your purchasing power is reduced 1s. 3d. per week. You were told in July last that it would be otherwise; you were led to believe that if there was a change of Government, and the farmers made more of their produce, you would get higher wages. No other evidence is needed of the foolishness of your conduct, as your past experience ought to have told you. It is only by having a good organization at your back that the farmers will ever pay you a higher wage, and there is nothing unnatural in that. The farmer is a merchant: he has your labour to buy, and he will always buy it as cheaply as he can. That is so long as our present individualistic system remains, and labour is used for the sake of profit-making.

Mr. Rew, the Assistant Commissioner on Agricultural Depression, said in his report, that if the labourers had never heard of a Union they would have had to put up with a less wage than 9s. or 10s. per week; but fortunately or unfortunately, Mr. Rew has not lived as long as some of us have; neither has he had the same experience as we have. There is abundant evidence that when the men in Norfolk were well organized they received a much higher wage, and that they did not get it until they did organize; and the fact does not indicate that economic forces rule the labourers wages. The facts are, then, that so far as the condition of the labourer is concerned, they will close the year 1895 worse than they began, that is to say so far as wages and their purchasing power is concerned; and Heaven only knows it was bad enough before. It is not many weeks since a labourer's wife told me that after she had bought flour and coal she had only sixpence left. I should like those who are constantly harping upon the comfortable conditions of the labourers to take a round with me once a week and get a glimpse into the labourer's cottage. They would be able to detect at a glance the amount of poverty which exists amongst the working classes. They would soon see there was not much waste in the labourer's kitchen. They would see that so far as the labourers having the best end of the stick their share in the business is very small. It is to be hoped that the working men will seriously consider the position, and endeavour in the near future to better it. I have spoken out the plain, cruel, honest truth; I hope it will have the desired effect.

Arch's Union was by now completely gone. My Executive was seriously considering winding up the whole[Pg 88] thing. The funds of both districts had become exhausted, as also had the central fund, hence the Union existed only on paper. They decided to let the matter remain a few weeks more, and commence another year if only on paper, and in the last issue of the Leader for 1895 appeared the following article by me:—

By the time this week's issue of the Weekly Leader appears the year 1895 will have passed away and 1896 will have been ushered in. It will do us no harm, especially the rural workers, to look at the condition of labour and ascertain, if possible, its true condition. We have constantly dinned into our ears that there has been such improvement made in the condition of the workers these last few years that there is nothing left to be done. We are told the life of the workers is all that can be desired. Now, in commencing to review the life of the toilers I have no wish to infer that there have been no improvements in the working classes; far from it, for the various political reforms that have been passed these last few years have had a tendency to give labour a stake in the country. But even these have not brought those unmixed blessings as many would have us believe they have. In fact, I think it can be shown that in some respects each political reform has had a tendency to fetter labour and somewhat enslave it, because these political reforms have left loopholes for the landlords and capitalist to tyrannize over them. With the enfranchisement came the system of letting the cottages to the labourers at a fortnight's notice, and by so doing instead of the enfranchisement of the people giving Labour a free hand, it bound Labour tighter; and the last great reform of 1894 has given the landlords and employers an opportunity of tyrannizing over the workers in such a way as was never dreamt of by the promoters of the Bill. Thus, instead of the government of our villages being in the hands of the people, it is in the hands of a wealthy clique—for the simple reason that the landlords are able to hold over the heads of the workers the threat of higher rents, and a few of the daring spirits who have come forward and voiced their fellows' wrongs have become marked birds for the aristocratic tyrants to shoot at. With these facts before us, I think it must be confessed that so far as the liberty and freedom of Labour is concerned, we have closed the year 1895 with Labour as fettered as ever, especially the unskilled portion of it.

There is much being said to-day in reference to the wages of the workers, and an attempt is made to prove that Labour is receiving far the largest share of the reward of human industry,[Pg 89] and that their poverty is due to the drinking and improvident habits of the workers. That statement I do not accept. Those who prefer that charge against the workers spend more money in gambling and drink in one day than the workers with large families have to live upon in a week. The wage of the agricultural labourers is at the rate of 10s. per week, and unskilled labourers in the town about 16s. 3d. This is far below a fair living wage. The conditions under which the workers live will not bear very close inspection; some of the hovels in which they live are not fit for human habitation. Scores of the hovels in which the workers live they are compelled to nail up sacks to keep the wind and water out. A poor women told me a few days ago that she had to set bowls all over the bedroom when it rained. Another told me during the sharp weather, when the family woke up in the morning, their beds were all covered with snow; yet those poor creatures dare not complain for fear they would have nowhere to hide their heads; and if we turn our attention to the towns we find the workers in just as bad a condition, if not a little worse. Their living is of the coarsest kind, in fact it is a marvel how they exist at all. These comments are not for the purpose of disheartening anyone, but to show our critics that the condition of the workers is far from what it ought to be. They are intended further to arouse, if possible, the workers from their apathy, and to make a strenuous effort in the new year to better their position, which can only be done by combination. There is I still a remnant of the once strong Unions left; these have done I their work for you labourers in the past. If, however, you think a better system can be found, then by all means adopt it and get organized. Your opponents are getting more desperate every day; capital is becoming more organized for the purpose of resisting the just demands of labour.

[Pg 90]

CHAPTER VIII
FAREWELLS

In the first week of December 1895, at the request of the Cromer District Liberal Association, I invited Mr. Arch to come to Cromer and address a meeting there. This invitation he accepted. Mr. Ketton presided. I was anxious to give the old man a good reception, and I obtained the services of the Cromer and Southrepps Brass Bands to play Arch from the house at which he was staying to the Lecture Hall. I met him at the station in the afternoon, and as soon as I took his hand I found he was broken-hearted and bitterly disappointed. Big tears ran down his face. I took him to the house of his host and we had tea together. Later we adjourned to another room by ourselves. Arch gripped me by the hand and said: "My boy, you are younger than I, therefore you will be able to return to work, but take my advice. When you do, never trust our class again. I am getting old, I have given all the best years of my life in their interest, and now in my old age they have forsaken me."

We had a splendid meeting, but he was not the same Arch he was in the days of the past. The bitter disappointment had affected him even on a political platform. I stayed with him that night and saw him off in the morning, feeling sure we should never meet again in a public capacity. We did not. At the General Election Arch retired, and his friends in the House of Commons,[Pg 91] irrespective of politics, subscribed and bought him a life annuity.

Early in the new year (1896) the directors of the Weekly Leader decided to wind up the company, as no advertisements could be obtained, and on February 8, 1896, the last issue of the paper was published. In it appeared my parting words to the labourers, and I did not fail to speak out plainly.

A PARTING WORD TO THE LABOURERS

Fellow Workers,

It is with deep regret that I write these comments this week, as this is the last issue of the Weekly Leader, the only organ in Norfolk that has for some time fearlessly advocated your rights. With its disappearance I shall have to vanish from public life too, and in order to make my position clear before the public I propose to give a brief outline of my connection with public movements, especially the Labour movement.

In 1884 and 1885, when the labourer became enfranchised, I was in a good situation as brick-burner. My employer was a Tory, but I held contrary opinions. Being a working man and Nonconformist, I had the courage to do what little I could for the party which I thought would best serve the working men and the country at large, hence I spoke at several of the Liberal meetings in Norfolk. For this I lost my work, and was turned out of my house, and was only able to get another by a man sub-letting to me. I was never able to get another place as brick-burner, and I turned to that of agricultural labourer, which I understood as well as the other work. But I was only able to do this by walking twelve miles a day, as no farmer in my neighbourhood would employ me. This I did for eighteen months. Then Mr. Ketton of Felbrigg Hall, my employer at that time, found me a cottage where I am now living. No sooner had I got settled in my new home than the working men, getting dissatisfied with their lot in life and having no labourers' Union, turned to me to help them to reorganize themselves. For some weeks I refused to take any part. Having been once boycotted and being now only just settled down under a liberal employer, I felt I had no further wish to bear the turmoils of public life; but at last through the men's constant appealing I yielded to their pressure. Eleven labourers formed a committee and waited upon me at my house[Pg 92] on November 5, 1889, and after they had decided among themselves what kind of Union they wished to start, I consented to act as secretary. I at once threw myself into the work, and in nine months enrolled in the Union upwards of 1,000 members, keeping at my work all the same time, holding meetings after I had done my day's work, many a time travelling twelve and fourteen miles to do so, and often not seeing my bed at all. At the end of nine months the committee decided that my whole time should be given to the work. I cautioned them and begged the men not to take me from my work, and for a time I refused to give it up. But at last, feeling that I must either give the movement up or give up my work, as my constitution was being seriously impaired, I yielded to the wishes of the men, and a general meeting was called to decide upon my salary. One pound a week was fixed, but I refused to take a pound whilst the men were being paid so low, and took 15s. per week only. About this time we became amalgamated with a Norwich Union, which was started about the same time as our Cromer Union, and in due time I became General Secretary, my salary being raised to 18s. per week. This amount I had for about eighteen months, when the men began to leave the Union, and now for several months I have had no salary at all.

Now for a short account of the work done. We found the labourers working for 10s. per week, which was soon raised to 12s., and in a number of villages to 13s. Their harvest wages were raised from £6 to £6 10s. to £7 and £7 5s. We also assisted a large number of the men to migrate and emigrate to other fields of labour. In 1892 I fought a spirited contest in a County Council Election at the express wish of the labourers themselves. At the passing of the District and Parish Councils Act I did my best to enable you to put it into operation. I have given this outline of my work and connection with working men's movements so that when my voice is silent, and my pen is still, and I go into obscurity, the public may be able to rightly judge of my work. One thing I can honestly say—in advocating the rights of the working men I have never studied my own personal interests or comfort. I have fearlessly championed your cause and have said and done for your interest what I have honestly believed to be right, and in doing so I have alienated those from me who would otherwise have been my friends, because in fighting your cause I have fought against their interests. I have in your interests made myself a bore to almost everyone, and have been a target for everyone to shoot at, while all through the work I have been grossly misrepresented. But none of these things have moved me, as I felt that I was fighting a noble and just cause. But alas! you the working men soon grew weary in well-doing, you allowed a spirit[Pg 93] of apathy to grow up amongst you, and what is still worse, you have allowed a spirit of mistrust and wicked prejudice to grow up amongst you. You have believed the vilest calumnies that have been uttered against the leaders of the movement by your enemies, hence your failure to emancipate yourselves. Leader after leader has fallen because when victory was within sight you refused to hold up their hands, and now you find yourselves to-day in a helpless state.

In taking my final farewell of you, let it never be said that George Edwards has left you. It is you that have left him. I was prepared at all costs to voice your interests, for I have as strong a faith as ever in the justness of your cause and the justness of your claims to live by your labour. But I have lost all faith that you will ever manifest manliness and independence enough to claim your rights. But should you ever again be prepared to assert your rights, I hope you will be able to find someone to lead you successfully on till the harvest of your rights is fully accomplished. In my parting words I will say to you as did Ernest Jones in one of his beautiful poems, because, although you cannot realize it, your cause will one day triumph. Fellow workers, farewell! It is not for me to get the work accomplished. I would have helped you, but ye would not. I will say to you:—

Sharpen the sickle; how full the ears
Our children are crying for bread;
And the field has been watered with orphans' tears
And enriched with their fathers' dead.
And hopes that are buried, and hearts that broke,
Lie deep in the treasuring sod:
Then sweep down the grain with a thunder-stroke,
In the name of humanity's God.

A week before this I had received an offer from the Executive of the English Land Restoration League to undertake a tour with one of their vans in Wiltshire in the coming season, commencing May 1st. This I accepted. As there were several weeks before the engagement commenced, a friend living at Sheringham, Mr. B. Johnson, offered to find me a few weeks' work. On Monday February 10th I went to work for him a disappointed man, having lost all faith that my class would ever be manly enough to emancipate themselves.

To add to this disappointment I lost my seat on the[Pg 94] District Council, the Rev. Mills leading by four votes. This exhibition of ingratitude on the part of the working men in my own village after all I had done for them during my term of office was enough to crush the spirit of any man, for I had brought to the old people in receipt of relief living in that parish alone over £20 in increased relief. I had also obtained some few acres of allotments. In any case I felt I could never take any more interest in the business so long as I lived there. At the election of the Parish Council I refused to serve again, and the Council fell into the hands of the farmers; and there it has remained ever since.

In May I commenced my lecturing tour. I travelled by road into the county, holding meetings every night on the way. During my tour I ran against the law. On September 30th I was summoned by the police before the Trowbridge bench of magistrates for an alleged obstruction of the highway by holding a public meeting on Vickers Hill, Trowbridge, on September 18th.

The ground on which the van stood was vacant and belonged to the Council. The amusing part of the business was that at the time I was supposed to be speaking and causing an obstruction I was more than half a mile from the van. The man I left in charge of the van had got impatient and commenced the meeting before the chairman and myself could return. It was a most amusing case. Superintendent Tyler was prosecuting, and when I stepped into the box he ordered me out again, as he thought I was one of the public and was going into the wrong seat. He did not know I was the defendant.

The campaign was most successful and pleasant, and I gained an experience that has stood me in good stead since. Several amusing incidents occurred during the campaign. At a place near Devizes I was addressing a large meeting, and a Tory continually interrupted with the remark: "You would not do it if you were not paid for it." Subsequently a man came on to the van[Pg 95] and informed me of my interrupter's mode of living. This he did without anyone else's knowledge, and it prepared me for the next interruption. I had not long to wait for the same remark, and I retorted: "And when I am paid I cannot afford to keep two wives as some people do." A shout went up—"That is what he does." Needless to say I had no more interruptions from that quarter. I was in the county twenty-six weeks, and although the work was successful from a propaganda point of view, it did not save the Union in the interests of which I was working, namely the Wiltshire Union, financed by Mr. Louis Anstie, for it died out within a few weeks.

In October of the same year I returned home and again settled down to work. I went to work for a few weeks with the late Mr. Benjamin Johnson as a general labourer, and in January 1897 I accepted a situation as a brick-burner with the late Mr. J. N. Neale of Baconsthorpe, who opened a brickyard at Beeston. I kept with him some years. In the same month I was elected unopposed to the Erpingham District Council, and for years I lost a day a fortnight from my work to attend the meetings without fee or reward. My wife also kept her seat for the parishes of East and West Beckham. I was soon put on to all the committees again. In March of that year I was sent by the Board as their representative to a Poor Law conference at Colchester and again to one at Norwich in

1898, and in 1899 I was sent by the Board to a conference at Ipswich and was deputed by them to read a paper on Old Age Pensions. After a lengthy discussion the Board passed a resolution in favour of these. Strange to say, same few years later, when the Government brought in its scheme, it adopted in the main the principles I had advocated in my paper, with the exception of the age and income limit. I did not recommend any income and I advocated sixty-five as the qualifying age.

[Pg 96]

In the same week I attended a Primitive Methodist conference at Ipswich and read a paper on Sunday-schools in the villages. In 1900 I was elected chairman of the Erpingham Sanitary Committee, a position which I held for ten years until I left the district. In 1902 my health failed. I had a serious illness and was obliged to give up the brick work. I moved to Gresham and went to work for a Mrs. Sharpen as an agricultural labourer. I intended to settle down as a labourer for the rest of my life, but fate ruled otherwise, and I seemed to be marked out for a different sphere. Against my own personal wish, in the spring of 1903 I received another pressing invitation from the Liberal Party to accept a position as a speaker. This I refused at first, but eventually accepted, with the understanding that I should return home once a fortnight to attend the Guardians' meetings. In the autumn of that year, after Mr. Chamberlain started his Tariff Reform campaign, I went with the newly formed Free Trade Union and kept with them until the General Election of 1906. During my work with this organization I helped in almost every bye-election, worked in almost every county and had many exciting experiences. But even in this capacity, although all Agricultural Labourers Unions had been defunct for some time, the Tory Party still continued their gross libellous attacks upon me. They printed the last balance sheets of the Unions, manipulated the figures in a scandalous manner and endeavoured to show that I had had all the money paid by the members, though they knew I had not received a penny. Hundreds of thousands of these leaflets were printed and spread broadcast. My opponents would get to know where I was addressing meetings and send men to distribute these leaflets at the meetings. In many counties men became so enraged at this treatment of me that when the man whose name was on the leaflets appeared on the scene he had on several occasions to beat a hasty retreat. In no case[Pg 97] did this move have its desired effect, as the great political upheaval of 1906 proved.

After the General Election of 1906 the Free Trade Union had no further employment for the speakers and they paid them no retaining fee. I returned home and again settled down to work as an agricultural labourer.

[Pg 98]

CHAPTER IX
RESURRECTIONS

No sooner was the General Election over (which brought about the greatest Tory defeat that that Party had ever experienced) than victimization became rife. Scores of men were victimized on mere suspicion, especially in Norfolk. The labourers appealed to me from all parts of the country to help them to form another Union for the agricultural labourers. The correspondence revealed most glaring cases of victimization. I will give a sample of what was happening. One correspondent told me that during the election a lady canvassed a man who had had not been to any meetings of either Party. He was a very quiet fellow and used rather quaint and witty sayings. When asked if he would promise to vote for the Tory candidate he quietly asked her if she could keep a secret? She replied that she could. He then said, "So can I," and gave no promise. Within a month this man received notice to leave his work on the plea that his employer was going to reduce hands, and a week later he received a week's notice to leave his house. This latter notice was put into effect. The man had a wife and five children, and a friendly publican let him have the use of his clubroom in which to live until he could find another house.

This was only one case out of many, and I might say that although these cases were well known, the Liberal Party took no steps to protect these men.

These matters were brought to my notice in February[Pg 99] and March 1906, and letters kept coming to me containing most pathetic appeals to form another Union. Why I was the one to be written to I attribute to the fact that I was the only one of the former leaders of the men taking any part in public life. The others were either dead or had retired into private life. Arch had retired, Z. Walker was dead and many of the others had gone. I had continued in public life, retaining my membership of the District and Parish Councils. Having again settled down to work, however, I did not feel disposed again to accept the turmoil of leading the men and shouldering the responsibility of forming another Union. I did not feel equal to the task, and, so far as I knew, there were no means of raising funds for such a gigantic undertaking. For some months I took no action and told my correspondents that, if anyone would come forward to accept the responsibility, I would place the benefit of my past experiences at his service, that I would not only join the Union, but would help him in every way I could, but that I could not at my age accept the responsibility. I had then reached the age of fifty-six. Further than that, I could not bring myself to believe that the labourers would ever again have the courage to assert their rights and demand by organization justice for themselves, their wives and children.

Still letters kept coming to me from all parts of the country, but more especially from Norfolk.

I do not think I should ever have taken any steps to comply with the requests but for the influence of my wife. One night I returned home from my work and read the usual batch of letters. I said to my wife: "I do wish these poor people could find someone to lead them. I don't feel equal to the task." Her reply was: "You must try. There is no one else who will."

I looked into that dear face as I wish I could to-day, and I pointed out to her what a lonely life she had led in the past and that it would mean the same to her[Pg 100] again in the future. Her reply was: "If you will make the effort, I will make the sacrifice."

This was indicative of the woman's noble spirit and the faith she had in the righteousness of the cause. I could hesitate no longer. I decided to take steps at once to call a conference, knowing full well the huge task which I was taking in hand. There had not been a shred of a Union amongst the agricultural labourers for ten years.

I have gone into considerable detail with this part of my story in an endeavour to combat the false charge that has been brought against me in certain quarters, that all through my long public life I was always looking for a soft job for myself and was always living on someone else without doing anything for it. I leave this to the judgment of my readers. I think they will agree that I have endeavoured to devote my whole life to the cause of my fellows.

In the first week in June I took steps to devise means of calling a conference. I first wrote to several Members of Parliament who were known to me, laid the matter before them and appealed for their help. Those to whom I addressed letters included Mr. (now Sir) Richard Winfrey, Mr. A. W. Soames, who sat for a considerable number of years for the division for which I had the honour of election in 1920, Mr. (now Sir) Robert Price, and Mr. George Nicholls. These gentlemen all sent donations, but some had doubts about the success of the venture. Mr. Nicholls and Sir Richard Winfrey not only sent donations, but promised to attend the conference when held and render all the help they could. Amongst other gentlemen I wrote to and who sent subscriptions were the Earl of Kimberley and Mr. Herbert Day of Norwich.

Altogether I received £10. I made arrangements to hold the conference at North Walsham in Norfolk, and[Pg 101] engaged the club room of the Angel Hotel for July 6th. I also provided for a tea for the delegates. We were to have the conference at 2 p.m. and a public meeting in the Market Place at 7.30 p.m., and I announced that Mr. Richard Winfrey, M.P., Mr. George Nicholls, M.P., and myself were to address the meeting. I also sent out invitations to the following: Mr. W. B. Harris, Sleaford, Lincolnshire; Mr. J. Binder, C.C., Cambridgeshire; Mr. Blyth, Suffolk; and the following in Norfolk: Mr. W. G. Codling, Briston; Mr. J. Sage, Kenninghall; Mr. H. A. Day, Norwich; Mr. Holman, Shipdham; Mr. Israel Lake, Gresham; and Mr. Baldwin, Cromer. All attended with the exception of the last.

At the opening of the conference Mr. George Nicholls, M.P., was voted to the chair and Mr. W. B. Harris to the vice-chair. After the chairman had welcomed the delegates, I was called upon to explain the objects of the conference. Before doing so I read several letters and went on to say that I had been asked to make another attempt to form a Union for the agricultural labourers. I explained that I thought a Union should be formed for securing for the labourers better conditions of living, assisting them to obtain allotments and small holdings, to secure better representation on all local authorities, and also representation in the Imperial Parliament, and that its funds should be used for these purposes.

The following is a brief extract from my speech:—

Gentlemen,—You have been called together to consider the advisability or otherwise of making another attempt to organize the agricultural labourers. The calling of the conference is also in response to a number of appeals from all parts of the Eastern Counties. I think the desire to form another Union is general and that the time is opportune for such an effort to be made. The men have been disorganized for over ten years, and in consequence their condition is no better than it was prior to 1872. But if such an effort is to be successful, one thing is essential. There must not be rival Unions. There must be one Union and one only, catering for the agricultural labourers. The many rival Unions[Pg 102] that were raised in Arch's days were, I have no doubt, a great factor in its fall. I think I ought to warn you that in forming such a Union you have a great task in front of you. One thing must be borne in mind. You cannot run such a Union on the same lines as Trades' Unions are run in large centres of industry. In consequence of the isolated condition of the labourers and the great distances to travel, the expense will be very great and, through the miserably low wage the labourer receives, the contributions he will be able to pay will be very small. Therefore accumulation of funds will be very slow. In my judgment it will take years to build up a Union that will be effective in altering the conditions of the labourer. But I have faith that it can be done, and in due course the labourer will be able to take his place with his fellows in the towns. One thing is certain, however. A great deal of hard work will have to be done by someone. Also great sacrifices will have to be made, and those responsible for the running of the Union will come in for a great deal of abuse.

A long discussion followed as to the best method to be pursued. Ultimately the following resolution was moved and carried:—

That this conference of agricultural labourers considers the time has come when steps should be taken to form a Union for the agricultural labourers, and that a provisional committee should be formed to carry this into effect.

Then the question of name arose. It was subsequently agreed that the name should be: "The Eastern Counties Agricultural Labourers' and Small Holders' Union."

Then followed a long discussion as to the objects, Mr. Day contending that they should be confined to the land question and that the Union should be run on much the same lines as the old Irish Land League. This was ruled out as being of no use to the labourer, and it was urged that if it was to be successful it must be a Trade Union in the fullest sense. This view was unanimously endorsed. It was also decided that the rules should be so framed as to enable the Union to assist the members to obtain land and let it to the members.

The conference then proceeded to elect a provisional[Pg 103] committee to act to the end of the year, this committee to use every endeavour to inaugurate the Union in the various counties represented at the conference. The following were elected to serve on the committee:—

President: Mr. George Nicholls, M.P.

Vice-President: Mr. W. B. Harris, Lincolnshire.

Treasurer: Mr. Richard Winfrey, M.P., Peterborough.

General Secretary: Mr. George Edwards, Gresham.

Executive Committee: Messrs. J. Binder, J. Sage, W. G. Codling, H. A. Day, J. Bly, C. Holman and J. Stibbons.

At the conclusion of the conference the delegates took tea together at the Angel Hotel. In the evening a large public meeting was held in the market-place, near the old cross. Mr. R. Winfrey, M.P., presided, and the meeting was addressed by Mr. George Nicholls, M.P., Mr. H. A. Day, and myself. We explained what had been done at the conference, and that we should visit the town again shortly with the object of forming a branch of the Union.

On going through the expenses of the day's proceedings I found that they totalled £11, having had to pay the delegates' rail fare, cost of room, tea and printing. I had received only £10 in donations, and thus I was £1 out of pocket on the day. It will be seen that I was left in a most difficult position from which to commence organizing the labourers.

At the conclusion of the conference Mr. Day suggested I should have to give all my time to the organizing work. I pointed out to him that that was impossible as I could not live without an income. Mr. Day then said that the work had got to be done, and he undertook to make himself responsible for the payment to me of 13s. a week for the first twelve months to enable me to give my whole time to the work. I realised this was meagre remuneration, as I should have to keep my niece at home to do the writing, whilst I went about forming[Pg 104] branches. Still, I knew if the movement was to be successful someone would have to make a sacrifice, and as I had set myself the task I agreed to do it.

I did it on these terms for the first year.

I cycled about six thousand miles during that year, which averaged some bit over one hundred miles per week, and for the first twelve months 13s. per week was all my niece and myself received for the work. She conducted the correspondence and kept the accounts and I spent five days in each week going about forming branches. I was not able to do much before harvest, but I was able to form the following branches: Kenninghall, Shipdham and St. Faith's. Kenninghall was started with thirty members, Shipdham with forty and St. Faith's with twenty-five.

On the very day the conference met at North Walsham, July 6, 1906, I was returned unopposed to the Norfolk County Council for the Buxton Division. The seat became vacant on the death of Mr. Charles Louis Buxton, who had represented the division ever since the Council was formed. Some of my friends insisted upon me being nominated and promised to pay all the election expenses. Mr. William Case of Tuttington was the other candidate, but he withdrew and I was returned unopposed. I was at once put on to the Small Holding Committee, in which work I was interested. My return caused a great flutter in the Tory camp, and they determined I should not be returned unopposed at the general election. At the general election of 1907 they put up Colonel Kerrison, who beat me by fifty votes. This proved my last defeat in seeking election to this Council.

53

As soon as harvest operations were completed I commenced work for the Union in all earnestness. During the interval the committee had been hard at work drawing up rules. I had a few copies of the rules of the old Norfolk[Pg 105] and Norwich Amalgamated Labour Union, and we first decided to adopt the principles contained therein. After careful consideration, and whilst anxious to run the Union on democratic lines, we came to the conclusion that the principles of the old Union would be impossible on the grounds of expense and the smallness of the contributions of the members. We decided on centralization, and by the time harvest was over we had got the rules printed and ready for registration and membership cards ready for use. We started our autumn campaign by a big demonstration at Peterborough, at which the speakers were Mr. John Ward, M.P., Mr. George Nicholls, M.P., Mr. R. Winfrey, M.P., and myself. During the autumn I confined my labours to Norfolk. My method of working was as follows: I would cycle out in the daytime into villages, engage rooms, fill in blank bills with which I had previously furnished myself and distribute them. I always billed meetings a week ahead. We had a very wet autumn in 1906 and many miles did I cycle in the pouring rain. I never missed a day in going out to arrange meetings and I never missed a single meeting. The meetings were well attended and very seldom did I fail to open a branch. I frequently had to act as my own chairman. After I had spoken and explained the rules, I then appealed to the men to join the Union. I soon found that the men I was then appealing to were of quite a different type to those we appealed to in the seventies. They were more thoughtful. Therefore the progress of the Union was not so rapid as in 1872, but it was a steady growth. I had a feeling from the first that its growth would be steady, but that it would attain a much greater strength than the defunct Unions, and that the work which it would be called upon to do would be of a far wider nature and of greater importance than that of the other unions.

From September 1st to December 31st I opened forty-nine branches with a membership of 1,500. As I look[Pg 106] back to-day to those weary months I often wonder how I stood the work, and my heart is sad when I think of the lonely life led by my poor wife. I used to leave home on the Monday morning, returning again on the Saturday evening. As soon as I reached home I retired to a little bedroom which I had cleared in my cottage for an office, and there would help my niece with the accounts and the week's correspondence. Then on the Sunday I would again be away from home, conducting services for the Primitive Methodists. I always made it a point never to let my public work interfere with my religious work. Besides addressing five meetings a week and attending to the Guardians and District Council work, I wrote a weekly article on the objects of the Union in the Eastern Weekly Press, the People's Weekly Journal and the Bury Free Press, and by so doing kept the Union well before the working people, which greatly assisted it.

I had not proceeded far before I experienced the same difficulty in finding branch secretaries as in the old days, and young men soon became marked men. Our first trouble of the kind arose at Ashill, Norfolk, where a young man was elected branch secretary. He was promptly told by his employer he must give up his office with the Union or leave his employment. In several other places pressure was put upon the men, which all added to the difficulties of my task. Nevertheless, with strong faith in the justness of the cause, I pushed on with the work.

The Union was received with ridicule by the farmers at the first, and they contended that its life would be short, for if Arch had failed, then George Edwards, with only a little local influence, must fail. They reckoned without their book, and by the end of the year they found that "old George Edwards" was more successful in his work than they had given him credit for.

[Pg 107]

CHAPTER X
SUCCESS AT LAST

At the end of the year the Provisional Committee was so satisfied with the success of my efforts that they decided to call a general meeting of the branches formed and to invite the branches to send one delegate each. It was left to me to make the arrangements, and Norwich was selected as the place of meeting in the first week in February. I engaged the large room at the Co-operative Institute. By the time this delegate meeting was held I had formed fifty-six branches with a membership of nearly two thousand. Fifty-six delegates, together with the members of the Provisional Committee, attended. After paying all expenses incurred during the five months, postage, printing of rules, that day's conference, etc., the treasurer was able to report a credit balance of £47 7s 5d. A statement to this effect was afterwards given to the new Executive Committee.

By the first week in February 1907 I had completed all the arrangements for the meeting, had the agenda printed, prepared the Financial Statement and also had my report printed. The meeting was most enthusiastic. Mr. George Nicholls, M.P., presided and gave a most inspiring address. My report was received with great enthusiasm, and the meeting then settled down to business. A resolution was moved "That this meeting of delegates from the newly formed Union thanks the Provisional Committee and the Secretary for their efforts to again organize the agricultural labourers and that[Pg 108] we at once form ourselves into a Union and accept the rules as drawn up by the Provisional Committee." The Council then proceeded to elect the officers and Executive Committee, and the following were elected:—

President: Mr. George Nicholls, M.P.

Vice-President: Mr. H. A. Day.

Treasurer: Mr. Richard Winfrey, M.P.

General Secretary: Mr. George Edwards, C.C.

Executive Committee: Messrs. Thomas Thacker, W. G. Codling, C. Holman, J. Stibbons, and J. Binder.

It was decided that I should receive no salary until the Union had been running twelve months. My niece, Miss Blanche Corke, was given an honorarium of £2 for her services during the period of the past five months. It was also decided she should receive 7s. per week in the future as assistant secretary.

As soon as this meeting was over I again set out single-handed on a most vigorous campaign, Mr. Thomas Thacker of East Dereham giving valuable aid in his district. By March 31st the balance at the bank stood at £150 10s. 3½d., which represented a saving upon the quarter's working of £104 2s. 10½d. I had enrolled during the quarter 436 members. The entrance fees amounted to £10 18s. 2d., as we only charged 6d. entrance fees and 4d. for youths under eighteen years. This spurred me on to even greater efforts. It was, however, playing very heavily on my health, besides the heavy organizing work. The work at home increased as the Union increased, and I frequently had to sit up nearly all night on my return home at the week-end, as the clerical work at home was more than my niece could do; for, while she was a good writer and fairly good at figures, she, like me, had had no training in book-keeping and we were neither of us clerks, and we had to devise our own methods in keeping the books, which was not the quickest nor yet the best method, and, as I had no organizing help, I was obliged to be from home five whole days.

[Pg 109]

As I look back on those days and the long hours I had to put in, never having an hour's rest, for I had to seize every moment I could to inform myself on all the current topics of the day, when getting my meals having a book or newspaper in front of me, arousing myself early in the morning and giving myself to the closest study, I often think the then Executive was anything but Trade Unionist. They were not only risking wearing my life out with no remuneration (of which I did not complain), but they were working my niece night and day for the miserable sum of 7s. per week, and they refused to let me have even an assistant organizer until April 27th. Still, I do not regret the sacrifice I made in the interest of humanity.

On April 27th the first meeting of the Executive was held at the Liberal Club, Peterborough, and so fast had the Union grown during the four months that the Executive was obliged to set on an assistant organizer. Mr. Thomas Thacker was appointed until July, at a salary of 25s. per week, but with no guarantee that they would continue the appointment after that date. This showed how cautious the committee were and that they did not intend to waste the members' money.

The appointment of an assistant organizer did not relieve me of any work, for I continued my own organizing work with the same vigour as before, and in addition I had to organize my assistant's work, which also added to the clerical work at home, and the Executive made no effort to give me any assistance at home. By July our contributions had increased from £116 9s. 11d. to £133 0s. 1d. We had enrolled during the quarter 350 members. The entrance fees received for the quarter ending July were £9 15s. 8d. Our balance at the end of July stood at £242 3s. 4d., which was a saving on the quarter of £91 5s. 9d.

The second meeting of the Executive was held at Cozens' Temperance Hotel, King's Lynn, on Saturday, August 3rd,[Pg 110] when I presented my second quarterly report as shown above. At this meeting Mr. Day, who had been responsible for my 13s. per week, said that he considered that the Union had got into such a position that he thought it ought to be able to pay its secretary, especially as the Executive was employing a whole-time organizer. It was then decided that I should receive a salary of 23s. per week and travelling and out-of-pocket expenses, and that my niece should continue to receive 7s. per week as assistant secretary. Thus ended my year's work for this Union. During the year I had cycled 6,000 miles, which was over 100 miles per week.

In spite of the hard work and the long weary miles I cycled on lonely roads, often late at night, still it was a pleasant year's work, as I felt I was building up an organization that would accomplish some great things for this long neglected class, and I never felt that I was engaged in a more divine work than I was then doing. I had enrolled during the year 6,379 members. We had taken in contributions during the two quarters we had been officially started £299 10s., and with the £46 7s. 5d. handed over by the Provisional Committee as a balance left over after paying all expenses with £63 7s. in donations from sympathizers, we had saved on the two quarters' working £242 3s. 4d., which I think everyone must admit was no discredit to me after the twelve months most strenuous work I had put in. But the year's work was not without its humorous side. At one crowded meeting I was addressing a man was present who was evidently primed up for his job with plenty of beer. He kept up a running fire of interruption. Some of the women present wrote on a big card: "Here is the fool of the fair who has sold himself to Bung." Then a number of strong young fellows pinned it on his coat and lifted him bodily on to the platform amidst the laughter and jeers of the audience.

At this committee meeting Mr. Thacker was re-engaged[Pg 111] at a salary of 25s. per week. Having now been appointed a paid official, I felt that the responsibility resting on me was great, being the chief official of the Union, and, as the committee had decided to meet only once a quarter, they had placed great power into my hands to deal with the various problems such as small disputes, lock-outs, victimization, accident, and all cases needing legal assistance. They also appointed Mr. W. E. Keefe of Norwich the Union's solicitor, before whom I was instructed to put all cases needing legal assistance. This I felt was power and responsibility that ought never to be placed upon one man, especially in an organization that was so rapidly growing, and besides it was making one man an autocrat, which I, as a democrat, strongly objected to. But the Executive were staunch economists and decided to keep the working expenses down to the lowest possible point and they determined it should be so. The one thing they closely scrutinized was the finance. My colleague Mr. Thacker and myself set out in all earnestness, each holding five meetings per week with good results. During the quarter I had several lock-out cases and victimization cases to deal with, which cost the Union several pounds. I also put several cases of accidents into the hands of Mr. Keefe which were successfully dealt with by him. I ought to say here that Mr. Keefe has been a most able and loyal solicitor to the Union. The Executive also decided that I should prepare a quarterly financial statement and present to them at their quarterly meeting and also send it to each branch of the Union.

The disbursement during the midsummer quarter was heavy owing to several cases of lock-out I was called upon to support. Nothing particular happened to cause much trouble during the autumn quarter. We enrolled 800 members and saved £127. Our balance stood on December 31, 1907, at £361 8s. 2d. At the fourth quarterly meeting held at Lynn, January 18, 1908, the Executive again became anxious about the cost of[Pg 112] management and appointed a sub-committee to draw up a scheme and report as to putting the Union on a safer and cheaper basis. They also decided that the General Council Meeting be held at Lynn on Saturday February 22nd, and I be instructed to make all arrangements. Further, that I be instructed to provide each delegate with lunch and pay him his rail fare together with 2s. for loss of time. I don't think this can be said to be extravagant, in fact to-day the Trade Union world would consider it very mean. I think what alarmed the committee was that the Tories had commenced their old game and had raked up the balance sheets of the old Union and were spreading them broadcast. They would get to know where I was advertised to speak and send a man to distribute the lying leaflets from house to house in the village. But the Executive need not have been alarmed, for the man whom they were vilifying had got the confidence of the labourers this time and they were not going to be disorganized by such libellous leaflets. Hence the more often the attack was made, the faster the Union grew. The General Council Meeting was held on February 22, 1908, in the Central Hall, King's Lynn, and my balance sheet showed that we had a balance in hand on December 31st of £457 3s. 9d., a saving since the Union was officially formed on February 4, 1907, of £410 16s. 5d., which no one can say was bad achievement out of 2d. per week contribution.

The following is an extract from my report:—

Fellow Workers,—In presenting to you my first balance sheet and report, I wish to thank you for the confidence you have placed in me during the year. Also to thank the officers and friends who have given me such valuable service in establishing the Union. Our worthy President, Mr. George Nicholls, M.P., has spared no effort to help us and has attended as many meetings as his parliamentary duties would permit him. Mr. Herbert Day has rendered able assistance.... During the year I have attended 183 meetings for the Union, and in addition to these meetings[Pg 113] I have attended 83 meetings in connection with my duties as Guardian and County Councillor. Mr. Thacker has addressed, since his appointment in March, 170 meetings and has cycled 3,240 miles. I have cycled since January over 4,000 miles, and since I commenced to organize for the Union in July 1906, over 7,000 miles.

We have received urgent appeals to visit other counties, but the committee up to the present have only permitted me to visit Lincolnshire and Cambridgeshire, outside of Norfolk branches. In these two counties have been formed:—Cambridgeshire: Friday Bridge, Leverington and Wisbech St. Mary's. Lincolnshire: Gidney Drove End, Gosberton, Holbeach, Sutton, Sutterton, Walpole St. Andrews, Gedney Dyke, Sutton St. Edmunds and Billingborough. In Norfolk we have made rapid progress during the year. We have been called upon to place a large number of cases in our solicitor's hands, which he has dealt with in a most able manner. In three cases he was able to effect a settlement which put into our members' pockets £236 12s. 6d. I think the Union ought to congratulate itself that it has such an able advocate as Mr. Keefe. Brethren, in closing my report, let me give you a note of warning. We are on the eve of a great social upheaval, the greatest the world has ever seen. It has already begun by the great Labour unrest throughout the industrial world. It is a proof that the workers are determined upon better conditions of labour. There is, however, a great fear that the capitalist class will use every means in their power to prevent the emancipation of the workers, and to be forewarned is to be forearmed. Alas! how often have we in the days of the past in our efforts to bind you together in the bonds of unity had to exclaim, like the prophets of old, "who have believed our report?" Our class has been contented for so long to be blinded by the capitalist class and has put too much faith in the political parties instead of thinking and acting for themselves. This spirit of apathy and childlike dependence must cease. You must think and act for yourselves and take an intelligent interest in all the great social problems that affect you as a class.

Considering all the opposition that we shall have to meet, it will require our united efforts to prevent the privileged class crushing the noble efforts that are now being made for industrial freedom. We are now celebrating the first anniversary of the establishment of our Union. Its progress has not been quite so rapid as some of us had hoped after the bitter experience of the rural workers during their disorganized state. We thought that it would have required very little effort to have organized at least 20 per cent., and it would not have been necessary to have spent a large amount of money and time. I was well aware by my past[Pg 114] experience that a great deal of opposition would have to be encountered, but the cost of organizing is certainly beyond my expectations. Notwithstanding all this, there is a good awakening, and I have strong faith that before many years our Union will become a great national movement, which certainly will be essential if the rural worker is to take his part in the social battle that is about to be fought.

You are the worst paid and worst housed and work the longest hours of any other class. While every other class have their holidays, you have none. The system under which you hire your cottages makes you complete slaves. Your poverty-stricken condition is a standing disgrace to a country that boasts of its high state of civilization and calls itself Christian. It is unjust and inhuman. This terrible curse and stigma will have to be abolished. It will, however, be a most arduous task. The battle will be fierce and long. Some of us may have to lay down our weapons of warfare before the battle is over, but it will have to be fought and the victory won. Take courage, then, my brethren, go forward with manly conduct, be sober, let your action be honest and straightforward to your employers, and your complete emancipation is assured.

> Courage then, my Brother,
> The day has come at last;
> The clouds are lifting quickly,
> The night is breaking fast.
> Be strong then of courage,
> Our cause is just and right,
> And he who holds by justice
> Is sure to win the fight.
> Yours faithfully,
>
> (Signed) George Edwards,
> General Secretary.

Gresham, December 31, 1907.

A resolution was passed adopting my report and balance sheet and a vote of thanks was given me for my year's work. The Council elected an almost new Executive. Mr. Petch was put on representing Lincolnshire, Mr. Arnett, Mr. Giles and Mr. Reeder were new members. A new spirit was infused by the election of the new members, but even these were afraid to launch out and engage more organizers and extend our borders[Pg 115] into other counties, but decided to confine my labours to the Eastern Counties. The new system of working the Union, however, increased the clerical work at home, as I was responsible for the mapping out of the districts for the superintendents and for keeping a record of their work. I was also expected to continue my organizing work as before, which I did. We made rapid progress, and by March 31st we had enrolled 700 new members during the quarter, and when the Executive met on April 25th I felt, unless there was speedily an alteration, I should soon have a serious breakdown, as the night and day work was telling on my health. It took my niece all her time to keep the accounts, hence I had to have all correspondence sent on to me day by day for me to answer, and, further, there were so many small cases of disputes and victimization that had to be investigated. The responsibility upon me was too great a mental strain, still I kept at it, as success was attending my work and it buoyed me up and kept me going. Still, the evil day had to come, and in June I broke down and had to take three weeks' complete rest. My niece was also on the point of getting married. The committee met to receive the report for the June quarter, the meeting being held in Lynn on July 14th. I was able to report that we had enrolled 1,040 members during the quarter and that we had added to our capital £175 during the quarter, and that our capital now stood at £632 12s. 6d. The committee decided to give me a free hand to do such work as I felt able to, with the understanding that the committee wished me to take sufficient rest to enable me to recoup my health. I took three weeks' rest from all public meetings. At this meeting the committee presented my niece with a case of knives and forks and an artistic address in recognition of her services to the Union. They also decided to increase my salary 5s. per week to enable me to secure another assistant. The joint salary of my niece and myself was 30s., 7s.[Pg 116] per week for her and 23s. for myself. Now I was to pay an assistant 12s. per week and I receive 23s. as before. My niece was married on August 4th. She and her husband, Mr. W. Painter, went to Lancashire to live, and Miss Alice Pike of Gresham entered the service of the Union as an assistant secretary. We still kept my small bedroom for an office, for which I never charged a penny. It was, however, being crowded out, and what the Sanitary Inspector would have said if he had made an inspection I often wonder.

At this time I received an application from the East Winch Branch secretary to hold a Sunday meeting on the common in that village. I objected, and only consented on the condition that the meeting should be of strictly religious character. This was agreed to, and on the last Sunday in July the meeting was held, and I advertised it as follows:—

Eastern Counties Agricultural Labourers'
and Small Holders' Union.

A Camp Meeting will be held under the auspices of the above on Sunday on the Common, East Winch. Services to commence at 2.30 and 6.30 p.m. Addresses will be given by C. Reynolds, George Edwards, General Secretary, and others. The Westacre Brass Band will be in attendance. Sankey's hymns will be sung.

It was a beautifully fine Sunday, and the services were attended by over 2,000 people. Such a sight had never been witnessed before in the village. The singing was most hearty, accompanied by the band. I took for my text in the afternoon "The labourer is worthy of his hire," and in the evening my text was "Thy kingdom come." The evening discourse was fully reported in the Lynn News. This caused a great stir. Some denounced it as mixing up politics with religion, others said they had never heard the Gospel preached like it before, and demands for Sunday meetings came in rapidly. Before the summer was over similar meetings were held at Wells,[Pg 117] South Creake and Swaffham, which were attended by thousands of people. The later meetings were addressed by Mr. George Nicholls, M.P., Mr. R. Winfrey, M.P., Mr. H. A. Day and myself. This was the beginning of the Sunday meetings, and so long as I was responsible for conducting them they were always conducted on strictly religious lines. We always opened with prayer and lessons from the Scriptures were always read. Large collections were received. So great was the interest taken in them that the committee decided to continue them in 1909. They also decided to have some Labour hymns of their own, and Mr. Day, Mr. Green and I were asked to make a selection. Mr. Green composed some of the most beautiful verses I have ever seen, and they were set to Sankey's tunes. I often wish the Union had kept them, for they have never found better. The following are a few of them:—

THE MODEL CHURCH.
(Tune: Sankey 608.)
Wife, I have found the Labour Church
And worshipped there to-day:
It's not like those so long we've known
Where parsons preach for pay.
But one that's built of human love
To bless the human race,
No church that ere before it stood
Filled so divine a place.
It's such a church that I, dear wife,
This very day have found.
There's no deception in its faith,
It stands on hallowed ground.
Ground sanctified by martyr's blood
Who o'er its surface trod,
When battling for their liberty
Their Conscience and their God.
Oh, come with me, I pray thee, wife,
And worship at its shrine,
Give thy adhesion to its Cause,
And make its interest thine,
[Pg 118]
Its songs are of the right to live
For every one who toils,
With their freedom of accession
To live upon the soil.
My heart grew restive at its words,
My spirit caught the fire,
I joined the utmost of my voice
To that most ardent choir,
And sang as in my youthful days,
Let tyrants prostrate fall,
Bring forth the honest man of toil,
And crown him, crown him, crown him.
Crown him best of all.

Come, wife, that fight will soon be o'er
The victory's nearly won:
The better land is just ahead,
I see its rising sun.
We're nearing now its happy shore,
Where streams of plenty run,
And there we'll never want again,
There'll be no sorrow there,
In that just land where all is love,
There'll be no sorrow there.

THE UNION LIGHT.
(Tune: "Stand up for Jesus.")
Stand up, the men of Labour,
Who toil upon the land,
For better homes and wages
Make one united stand.
Your captains, they will lead you,
If you will follow on,
Now is the time, O comrades,
Haste age to come along.

STRONG HUMAN LOVE
(Tune: "Lead, Kindly Light.")
Strong, human love! within whose steadfast Will
Is always peace.
O stay with me, storm-tossed on waves of ill;
Let passions cease.
Come thou in power within my heart to reign.
For I am weak and struggle has begun.
[Pg 119]

This book, which contains some of the finest phrases with twenty-six songs, was used for years at our meetings as our official hymn-book, but after a time it was revised and in my judgment some of the best hymns were left out. Still, I must not complain, as young folks are anxious to keep up to date.

The committee at their last meeting took the step of forming Conciliation and Arbitration Councils, and they decided to move the following resolution at the General Council Meeting:—

That the Executive be authorized to endeavour to form Conciliation and Arbitration Boards for the area in which the Union works. On such Boards the employers and labourers be equally represented and an outside Chairman be appointed, and they shall have power to consider all questions in this area of wages and conditions of work and for the immediate future. Pending the carrying out of this, the Executive Committee be instructed to request the Farmers' Federation to agree to a rise of 1s. per week from March next.

So far as this resolution was concerned the Farmers' Federation refused to meet us. It was, however, evident that the men were getting restless, and I could see that unless the

Farmers' Federation were prepared to meet us there would be a grave danger of a serious outbreak in the near future. We closed the year 1908, however, with a balance of £997 18s. 6d.

In September 1908 Mr. Rippingall of Langham died and a vacancy was caused in the Walsingham County Council Division. At the request of the members living in this district and with the permission of the Executive I was put forward as a Labour candidate. This time I decided I would run purely as an independent Labour candidate, and that I would have nothing more to do with either political party. I had all my bills printed in the Union colour, green. I also used the motto I selected for the Union: "Be just and fear not." I[Pg 120] fought the election single-handed. I acted as my own agent and arranged my own meetings, the only assistants I had being my colleague Mr. Thomas Thacker and Mr. Robert Green. My assistant did the clerical work. We addressed all the envelopes, folded all the addresses ourselves and posted them. We had meetings in every parish in the district. The labourers were very enthusiastic. I soon found the leading Liberals were most anxious to find some excuse to vote against Labour in spite of what I had done for the party in North Norfolk. The excuse they found was no party politics in County Council elections. Yet, strange to say, my opponent Mr. Walker and his agent were strong Tories. No one thought I stood a shadow of a chance as a direct Labour candidate. The contest lasted three weeks and it was a most strenuous fight. My colleague Mr. Thacker and myself worked night and day. We threw all our strength into the contest, holding meetings and addressing envelopes during the day. As the election drew near we realized it would be a close contest. My opponents were confident that they were winning. On the day of the election the farmers and tradesmen rallied up to the support of my opponent. Every available conveyance was brought up to his support and all my supporters had to walk. Many had to walk three and four miles to vote after they had done their day's work, but did it cheerfully, many going to vote before going home to tea. At the close of the poll everyone realized it was a very close fight. Even the Tories were not so sure that they had won. I appointed my colleague and Mr. H. J. Gidney, who rendered valuable help during the election, as my counting agents. The counting of the votes was done in the Returning Officer's house, and then for the first time I found out that his son was my opponent's agent and had been acting as Deputy Returning Officer. To this arrangement I raised the strongest protest. The counting was most exciting; we kept side by[Pg 121] side all the time, and at the close the Returning Officer declared we had tied. We were not satisfied and demanded a recount, and, further, the number of votes did not correspond with counterfoils. The result of the recount left us as before. Still, there were four papers short. At this stage the keen eye of my colleague detected four papers under the looking-glass, and these four votes were mine. None knew how the ballot papers got under the glass, but they were there and were mine, and I was declared elected. My opponents were indignant, and protested that when the general election for the Council came their candidate would fight again. But this the poor man was not allowed to do, for within three months after this contest he was taken seriously ill and died.

At the yearly meeting in March 1909, when the election of the committees took place, I was put on to the Small Holdings Committee, Public Health Committee and Old

Age Pensions Committee. These committees I felt more deeply interested in. The first was a movement which the Union had made a part of its object.

On squaring up the accounts of the election I found that it had cost £3 19s., which was caused by hire of rooms, printing and postages.

I was the first direct Labour representative elected on to the County Council, and, being free from any political ties, I felt myself free to take any action I thought was best in the interest of the class I directly represented. I devoted most of my energies to the working of the Small Holdings Act. I soon found, however, we were up against a big problem and that land was not so easy to get as I had thought it was before I was a member of the committee. The Act was surrounded with so much red tape and the landlords' interests were safeguarded at every turn, which enabled them to put obstacles in the way and make it most difficult to obtain land that we could let to the men at reasonable rents, and our progress was very slow. Hundreds[Pg 122] of applications for land were sent in, varying from five acres to fifty, especially after my election, as they apparently thought I, being a Labour member, would carry everything before me. Apparently they thought that we had nothing to do but to go and take the land and buy it in the same way as we go and buy any other article. Hence hundreds of men got tired of waiting. But we made good progress, and by October 1909 we had obtained over a thousand acres of land and put over 115 men on to the land.

At the general election of the Council in 1910 I moved from the Walsingham District to the Free Bridge Lynn Division, according to the promise I had made previous to my going to Walsingham at the bye-election. This time I was fighting a sitting member and one of the largest farmers in Norfolk. I again stood as a direct Labour candidate. This time I had less help than before, as my colleague was fighting the Litcham Division for a seat on the Council and Mr. Robert Green was fighting the Walsingham Division which I had left. The only helper as a speaker was my old friend Mr. Thomas Higdon, the hero of the Burston School Strike. The contest was a sharp one. My opponent had the help of several of the members of the Council, both Liberal and Tory, who were being returned unopposed. This contest nearly knocked my assistant Miss Pike and myself up, but in spite of the number of speakers brought into the division, I won the election by a majority of eighty. I had, however, in this contest a good deal of local help from amongst my own people, as we were better organized in this division, notably Mr. Matthew Berry of East Winch and Mr. James Coe of Castleacre.

At the first meeting of the new Council I was put on to the following committees: Public Health, Mental Hospital, Small Holdings, Old Age Pensions, Western Highways. From this moment I was treated with the greatest amount of respect by every member of the[Pg 123] Council and listened to with interest. I set myself to work diplomatically to accomplish the things for which I was sent there, for I found on going into the Mental Hospital, although the problem of dealing with those mentally affected is a pathetic one, still to me it was pleasant work, as it touched my humanity, and I found Dr. Thompson, the Medical Superintendent, most human and kind, and beloved by all brought into contact with him. I found also that whilst demanding strict discipline, as he must do, still to his staff he was most fair and always willing to listen to a grievance. I have had to discuss matters with him at different times as the Trade Unions' representative on the committee, and I am pleased to say we have been able to make many improvements in the working conditions of the staff since I have been on the committee. About this time they were engaged in erecting a nurses' home. This completed, we then pushed through another scheme, new stores and hall which is used for balls and entertainment for the inmates and staff. I am pleased to say that every comfort for these poor unfortunate creatures is studied. I have had to put up one fight since I have been on the committee in connection with the dietary. I fought most strenuously the question of margarine, but got defeated.

The Small Holdings movement made rapid progress. I soon found this added considerably to my labours. It meant nearly two days per week, and with my District Council and Board of Guardians work I was very heavily harnessed with local government work. It was, however, educational and interesting. About this time I was elected Chairman of the Erpingham Rural District Council Sanitary Committee, but I used to so arrange my Union work that I never neglected one of their meetings.

[Pg 124]

CHAPTER XI
UNREST

On February 20, 1909, the third General Council Meeting of the Union was held in St. James's Hall, King's Lynn, and by the resolutions that were sent in from the various branches I was satisfied that the men were getting restless and that without great care trouble was facing us in the near future, and that it was imperative that we should be taking some steps to secure some improvement in the working condition of our members. The committee, however, could not see that there was any danger; but I could see it, and I did persuade the Executive to allow me to write to the Farmers' Federation and invite them to meet us and discuss the question of some readjustment in wages. This I did, but it was again refused. On receipt of this refusal the Executive passed a resolution at their meeting held on April 24th that Mr. Nicholls and Mr. Winfrey be requested to take steps to have the agricultural labourers included in any scheme of arbitration that might be formed. They also instructed me to write every branch that when they desired increase in wages they must communicate with me and that I would suggest what action was to be taken, and that I was to advise all members to sign a paper requesting a rise, and that I be instructed to enclose the same and forward it to each employer. Here were more superhuman responsibilities placed on my shoulders, making me absolutely responsible for every trouble that might arise. As I look at these old minutes[Pg 125] that were passed, without complaining of the action of the Executive, I sometimes wonder what kind of man the Executive thought I was. They must have thought I was superhuman, which I was not by any means, for I had very serious limitations. Never before had any one man such grave responsibilities put upon him, and I knew it and it worried me beyond degree. But I faced the work with great faith in the eternal resources and trust in Divine help.

I had, however, one great trouble. My dear wife, who had been such a help to me, began to fail in health, both mentally and bodily, and I saw the end was coming. During the summer it was my misfortune to be insulted by a drunken man, a son of a small farmer at Sharrington. I was advertised to address a meeting near the old cross at Sharrington. On my arrival at the place of meeting this man lay on the green drunk. As soon as I commenced to speak he commenced to brawl and shout so that no one could be heard. When I asked him to be quiet he got up and struck me a violent blow in the chest. What else he would have done had he not been stopped I am unable to say. As it was I was laid up for a week and had to go to a doctor. The man was summoned before the Holt Bench and he was fined £1.

The Executive at the meeting held on April 24th decided that the Union should be affiliated with the Trade Union Congress, and that we should pay on the basis of 3,000 members. I was elected delegate to attend the Congress at Ipswich on September 6th, which I did, and had a most cordial reception by the delegates and was especially mentioned in the President's address. I attended the Congress and spoke on the system of tied cottages. Mr. Smillie, on behalf of the miners, moved the following resolution:—

This Congress urges upon the Labour Members in the House of Commons to take up at once the question of the eviction of[Pg 126] workmen and their families from their homes during trade disputes and do everything possible to pass into law a measure that would put an end to this cruel method of warfare.

Although this resolution did not quite meet the case of the agricultural labourer, I supported it, as it gave me an opportunity to bring before the public's notice the difficult position the tied cottage system put the agricultural labourers in. I made the following speech:—

The delegates coming from the large centres of industry have no idea of the seriousness of the question from the standpoint of the agricultural labourers. If a town worker is evicted from his house he can soon get another in an adjoining street. That is not the case with the agricultural labourer. If he is evicted from his cottage he cannot get another in the same village nor in any of the five or six villages near him. I hold in my hand a copy of an agreement which an agricultural labourer has to enter into with the landlord on some estates before he takes his cottage. It reads as follows:—

"I, the undersigned, agree to hire the cottage in the Parish of................the property of..................at a rental of................and agree to give the cottage up at a week's notice should the landlord require it for any other workman.

I also agree not to keep any pigs or fowls without first obtaining permission from the landlord or his agent.

I will also act as night-watchman when required, and give any information I may have that will lead to the conviction of anyone seen poaching on the estate.

I also undertake not to harbour any of my family who may misconduct themselves in any way.

I also agree on leaving my cottage to hand over my copper and oven to the landlord or his agent and not to disturb the bricks or to remove these utensils until the landlord or his agent have refused to purchase them.

I will also undertake to live at peace with my neighbours and to lead an honest and respectable life.

I will, before admitting any of my family home, apply to the landlord or his agent for permission, giving particulars on a form provided by the landlord, their names and ages, also if married or single, and how long they want to stay."

That is the kind of agreement agricultural labourers are called upon to sign. It shows the Congress the nature of the difficulties[Pg 127] that confront agricultural labourers. You might say the labourers are not intelligent enough to combine: they are intelligent enough if they have the freedom. Only this week, since I have been at this Congress, I have received a telegram from our solicitor who is contesting a case before the Grimston Bench on behalf of the Agricultural Labourers' Union. It relates to a labourer who obtained permission for a holiday. But when he went back to work he was discharged and received a week's notice to leave his cottage. He could not get another, and an ejectment order was applied for. Our solicitor in his telegram says the magistrates would have granted the ejectment order, but he was able to defeat it on technical grounds. This poor man's wife is within a month of her confinement, and, had the ejectment order been granted, his wife and four children would have been thrown on to the road. I ask you to do all you can to bring this matter to an issue and see if a Bill cannot be brought into Parliament giving the agricultural labourer security of tenure. Labourers who live under conditions such as I have described can neither make applications for allotments nor yet serve on local authorities. If they attempted to do such things, they are marked men and are turned out of their cottages at a week's notice. I trust that the cruel eviction business will soon become a thing of the past.

After some further discussion the resolution was carried unanimously, and for the first time the system under which the labourer has to hire his cottage was brought before the public. It has been a hardy annual at the Trade Union Congress ever since.

This exposure caused a tremendous sensation throughout the country. For months I was inundated with letters asking for the names of estates. Others sought for information for the purpose of writing articles in the press. It gave a wonderful impetus to the Union.

During the summer I held a number of Sunday services under the auspices of the Union. After I had addressed one of these meetings a rather exciting incident happened. When attending a meeting in a village in Norfolk a clergyman was at the meeting and expressed a wish to speak privately to me, and we adjourned to a room in the inn. On entering the room he said he had heard that I had been blaspheming the name of Jesus and[Pg 128] demanded that I make an apology to him (the clergyman). I told him I had done nothing of the kind, and, so far as apologizing to him, he would be the last man I should apologize to. Whereupon he informed me he was a lightweight champion boxer, and if I did not there would be bloodshed, and he came towards me. I at once pushed him over and left the room and went back to the meeting and reported what had taken place. Needless to say he had very soon to leave for his own safety.

During the autumn it became evident to me that trouble was looming in the near future. Numbers of small disputes took place, which I had to deal with on my own responsibility and which caused a good deal of anxiety.

As we approached the end of the year the branches were asked to send in resolutions for the General Council. Most of them were demanding that the Executive should take up the question of an increase in wages, Saturday half-holiday and a forty-eight hour week. At the December Executive I again warned the Executive that I feared we should soon have to face trouble as I was sure the members would soon press for an increase in consequence of the rise in the cost of living. I urged them to allow me to call them together at any time to discuss the best method of grappling with the situation and to obtain the increase so long delayed.

But they seemed to think I was able to deal with the situation. The General Council of the Union was not held in 1910 until March 19th. It was held in the Central Hall, King's Lynn. The reason for the Council meeting not being held until March was the General Election in January and the County Council Election in March. This Council Meeting was attended by nearly one hundred delegates. The greatest interest was taken in the proceedings. There were many resolutions on the agenda dealing with hours of labour and wages.[Pg 129] The resolution dealing with Saturday half-day was warmly debated and a resolution carried that the new Executive be instructed to take steps to secure the Saturday half-day, one journey all the year round and an increase of 1s. per week at once. At the close of the Council a short meeting of the new Executive was held. Mr. George Nicholls presided. I again pointed out to them the seriousness of the situation and told them I was sure there was trouble looming in the near future, and that the labourers, so far as Norfolk was concerned, would insist on an attempt being made for an increase in wage and an improvement in their working conditions. I urged them to give me more help and to allow me to bring them together at any time, even by wire if necessary; but this they refused and held that I was quite able to deal with any dispute that might arise without calling the committee together. The fact was that, while I had an Executive who were able and earnest and anxious to do their best to build up the Union, they were inexperienced so far as Trade Unionism was concerned. They were always anxious to keep working expenses down. At the committee the night before the Council the Treasurer, Mr. Richard Winfrey, wrote complaining about the increased expenditure during the year for organizing work, although we had saved during the year 1909 £503 11s. 8½d. and had only spent £771 9s. 9½d. out of a total income of £1,275 1s. 6d. This expenditure was for lock-out pay, postages and rent of rooms. Salaries paid during the year were for my assistant secretary, Miss Pike, and myself £91; divided as follows: Miss Pike 12s. per week, £31 4s.; myself £1 3s. per week, £59 16s.; my assistant organizer, Mr. Thomas Thacker, £1 5s. per week, £65. Total salaries for the three of us £156. Yet the Treasurer, in his anxiety to save money, thought this was too high an expenditure. Probably as an economist he was right, but no one can say that those who did the work were overpaid.[Pg 130] I left the Executive and the General Council on March 19, 1910, with a very heavy heart, for I could see by the temper of the men that they were determined within a very short time to press for an improvement in their conditions of living and in my judgement they were justified. In fact, it was long overdue, for the cost of living was rapidly rising, and I also knew that the farmers, as they had done in the days of the other Union, would fight this honest desire on the part of the labourers to its bitter end. The saddest thing for me was I could not get my Executive to see it and they left me to face it single-handed. But I set to work to prepare for the inevitable whenever it did come. I was determined to put my back against the wall and stand by the men, and at the same time to do all I could, whenever the trouble did arise, to bring the two sides together.

I had not long to wait. On April 5th I received a letter from Mr. Harvey, the secretary of the Trunch Branch, informing me that his members objected to working ten hours a day unless they received a rise of 1s. per week, a not very extravagant demand. I saw at once that the trouble I had for so long tried to impress upon my Executive had arrived, in fact I felt convinced the farmers were anxious to try their strength. On receipt of the letter I at once wrote to the branch secretary, instructing him to call a special meeting of his members for April 11th and at the same time telling him that no action must be taken until I had met them and obtained full particulars and laid them before the Executive, for in spite of what the Executive had done I was determined I would not take on my shoulders the responsibility of a strike without the Executive being called together to decide it and take their share of responsibility. I received no further information during the week, and I expected nothing would take place until I had an opportunity of meeting the men and discussing the[Pg 131] matter with them. But to my surprise on Monday April 11th I saw in the Daily Press that the men had struck work. Altogether thirty men were affected. It appears that the farmers had forced a lock-out by refusing to withdraw the notice until the men had time to meet me and discuss the matter with them. I was, however, determined to prevent an open rupture if possible. On Monday April 11th I attended the Erpingham Board of Guardians, of which the Secretary of the Farmers' Federation was deputy clerk. During the day we had an interview, and I promised that if he would prevent the importation of Federation labour I would try and persuade the men to go back to work until representatives of the two organizations could meet and come to some arrangement, he undertaking to persuade the farmers to reinstate all the men without prejudice. This he did. I, with Mr. Robert Green, Mr. W. Codling and Mr. Herbert Day, met the men at Trunch in the evening and thoroughly discussed the cause of the dispute with them. The facts were as follows: In March, as was the custom, the farmers requested the men to work ten hours a day. This the men agreed to on condition that the employers would give them an increase of 1s. per week. This the employers refused to do and gave the men a week's notice to leave unless they worked the ten hours, the men accepting the notice, which expired on April 8th. I advised the men to go back to work until the committee could meet and some arrangement could be made in reference to their hours of labour and conditions of work. This the Knapton men agreed to do, and on Tuesday morning I received a report that the Knapton men had gone back to work on a nine-hour day. I at once wrote to Mr. J. T. Willis the following letter, which will show how anxious I was to avoid a dispute and to meet the farmers, which I regret to say the farmers for years refused to do.

[Pg 132]

Flitcham,
April 10, 1910.

J. T. Willis, Esq.,
    Secretary, Farmers' Federation,
Sheringham.

Dear Sir,

I was pleased to hear from my representative at the Trunch district before leaving home this morning that some kind of a truce had been arranged between the employers and their men, which I think is a credit to both parties concerned; but to avoid any unpleasantness in the future and in order to arrive at a settlement that will be satisfactory to both parties, I beg to suggest to your committee that a committee be formed consisting of an equal number of employers and employed without prejudice to any one, with you and myself in addition, to represent the two organizations and discuss the whole question of hours and wages. I have hurried my committee on, and they will meet on Monday April 18th, probably at Sheringham, when the whole question will be discussed from our point of view. I shall be glad to hear from you before that date in reference to the above suggestion, and hope the truce will be maintained until after that date.

Yours faithfully,
(Signed) George Edwards,

General Secretary,
Agricultural Labourers' and Small Holders' Union.

To this letter I received no reply, but I heard from my representative during the week that the farmers had broken the truce and were again demanding that the men should work a ten-hour day, which they resolutely refused to do. When the men at Trunch met me on Saturday April 16th I found them all out again and very indignant at the treatment they had received from the employers. I soon found that all hope of a settlement was gone. The meeting was largely attended and most enthusiastic. I had never before witnessed such a spirit of determination. I addressed the men in a most hopeful tone, although in the first instance they were a little out of order. A resolution was passed without a dissentient voice urging upon the Executive to support them, and thus the trouble began.

[Pg 133]

My first effort to effect a settlement by peaceful means had failed. I could plainly see what was in front of me. I knew that the brunt of the battle would fall on me and I should have poured on my head showers of abuse and the grossest misrepresentation. But I knew the men's cause was just and their demands moderate, and I made up my mind I would fight their battle honestly and justly. The Executive met on Monday April 18th and decided to support the men to the utmost.

The struggle commenced in earnest. The men set themselves to it like grim death. The farmers became furious. The Farmers' Federation imported non-unionists into the villages, but no one would lodge them, so the farmers had to make provision for them. These men were not many of them efficient workmen. They received 10s. per week more than the labourers had asked. They also had lodgings free and a cook found to look after them. They were also supplied with plenty of beer. Policemen were sent into the village to keep order, as they said, but there was no need for it. For one thing I had pressed on the men that they must conduct the dispute in a peaceful way and not on any account allow themselves to be provoked into breaking the peace, for if they did I would not lead them. They received many provocations, but with no avail. Many threats were thrown out to them. The women dressed up an effigy and set it up in their garden and made its legs black, and wrote on it "blackleg." This the police ordered them to take down. I came into the village at the time and told the police to mind their own business or I should report them. No more was heard of it. Many attempts were made to evict these men from their houses, but failed. One thing in the men's favour was that Mr. Bircham of Knapton was under notice to leave his farm. It was up for sale. I was on the County Council and a member of the Small Holdings Committee. I advised these men to make an application to the County[Pg 134] Council for a small holding, which many of them did for five, ten, and even up to twenty acres, and so great was the demand that, when the farm was put up for sale, the Small Holdings Committee was one of the bidders and bought it. When this became known the farmers became more furious than ever.

I, of course, came in for all the credit for this and they were not far wrong. I look upon this as one of the best pieces of work I have been able to do for my people. So angry did the opponents of the men become that they became threatening in their attitude towards me, so much so that the men would insist on acting as my bodyguard when I went into the district, and it would have been a sorry day for any man who dared to have attempted to molest me. I set myself at once to collect funds to enable me to pay the men that had families more than strike pay, which was 10s. per week. The subscriptions came in fast. Our first collection was at a meeting held on a Sunday at Knapton when over a thousand people were present. The meeting was addressed by myself, Mr. Day, Mr. Robert Green, Mr. Thacker, and in the evening some friends came over from Norwich, amongst them being Mr. W. R. Smith, now the able President of the Union. This was the first time we had met and we soon became fast friends. The result of the day's collection was over £7 10s., and thus a good start was made. The men themselves were in fine form. This meeting did the greatest good in every respect. It awakened a spiritual interest such as there had not been for a very long time. I devoted my time during the week to holding public meetings and making collections for them. I never missed a Saturday night in going over to pay the men. This, however, meant many a long weary night cycle ride and long hours for my poor assistant at home. But the worst had yet to come. The struggle continued all the summer, and I don't think any one man suffered a penny loss. All the applicants[Pg 135] for small holdings and several of the men who had been locked out became tenants in October on the very farm on which they had been locked out a few months before. All of them were allowed to keep in their houses, so that we were able to find work elsewhere for those that could not take any land. Thus in this district, although the dispute lasted over six months, we won a notable victory and its effects are felt to-day, for the Trunch Branch is one of our largest branches in the Union, and Mr. Harvey, their first branch secretary, is still their secretary, and is to-day a member of the Norfolk County Council and a Justice of the Peace. In this district we have a fine type of the Norfolk labourers.

[Pg 136]

CHAPTER XII
THE GREAT STRIKE

On April 25th I got the committee together again. This time they met in the Cozens' Temperance Hotel, King's Lynn. There attended the following: Mr. George Nicholls, M.P., President; Mr. Richard Winfrey, M.P., Treasurer; Messrs H. Day, J. Stibbons, T. Thacker, W. Codling, A. P. Petch, G. Giles, M. Berry and myself. The first minute that was passed was that my quarterly report be received and that my action in giving support to the Trunch members out on strike be endorsed. The last part of the resolution was not necessary as the Emergency Committee I had called together on April 18th had decided that I should support the men, but it was an attempt on the part of some who were not at the meeting on the 18th to ignore the Emergency Committee, as they were opposed to my calling the meeting; but I stuck to my guns and said I would do it again if such an occasion arose. The malcontents, however, were determined I should not, so they passed the following resolution on the motion of Mr. Winfrey:—

That an Emergency Committee be formed consisting of the officers of the Union and three other members of the Union living nearest to the District where any dispute takes place, and that they have power to deal with any dispute that may arise and report the same to the next Executive Committee.

I warned them of the folly of such a resolution and told them that we were within measurable distance of[Pg 137] another dispute of much greater magnitude than the one we had got on at the moment. I asked them if they thought it was right for one or two men to commit the Union to a strike? No one knew where it might end. The reply I received was that they were not going to the expense of calling the committee together more than once a quarter. Mr. Day, who was in close touch with the enormous amount of work that was being heaped upon me and my assistant and knew that we were utterly unable to cope with it, moved a resolution that another organizer be appointed in order that I might devote more time to office work. This was turned down, although the Union was going up by leaps and bounds, which all added to the work of the Union, and we were left to struggle on as best we could. Can it be wondered at that the matters at the office got into a state of chaos? For it was humanly impossible for any one person to grapple with the work, especially in a room four feet by six feet and I never at home.

Events soon proved how true my forecast was, for on May 10th I received a letter from Mr. George Hewitt, branch secretary St. Faith's Branch, informing me that there was a great deal of unrest in the St. Faith's district in reference to the hours of labour and rate of wages and urging me to go over and hold a meeting and discuss the matter with them. I at once summoned a special meeting of the branch for May 14th. I also summoned Mr. H. A. Day, Mr. Robert Green and Mr. Thomas Thacker, members of the Executive, to an Emergency Committee according to the minute passed at the last Executive Committee.

All of them attended. The branch room was packed, every member being present. Mr. G. E. Hewitt presided. I asked the members to state definitely what alteration they required and what demands they wanted to have made on the employers. Their reply was that they wanted 1s. increase on their present wage, which would bring[Pg 138] their wages up to 14s. per week, and wished to have their hours of labour so arranged that their working week should finish at one o'clock on Saturdays. I could not say this was an unreasonable demand, in fact I had made the one o'clock stop on Saturdays one of the chief planks on my platform ever since the days of Arch, and so far as the rise of wages was concerned I felt it was long overdue. The labourer had not had an increase in wages for years, yet the cost of living had been steadily going up meanwhile. But the temper of the men was of such a nature that I felt the utmost caution must be exercised by us who were responsible for the conduct of the men and in whose hands the interest of the

Union was placed, for I felt that one false step would wreck the whole movement. The spirit of the men was so aroused that they demanded prompt action, which meant notices being handed in at once. This I knew would never do good, and I then proceeded to address the members in a speech in which I felt the grave responsibility resting upon me and which was delivered with some emotion. I counselled the men to move slowly and not to rush into any action without well considering the importance of such a step. And further, I told them that so far as I was concerned I could not consent to a strike until every other means of a peaceful nature had been tried and failed. I told them that if they consented to this course being taken, then, if we failed and the worst had to come, I would fight for them to the bitter end and would be a staunch advocate of their claims which I knew to be just. This rather damped them, and I do not think according to the temper the men were in that they would have allowed any other man to have said such things or have taken such an action. But I had the satisfaction of knowing that they thoroughly trusted me and would take any advice I thought it wise to give them, and I was able to persuade them to pass the following resolution:—

[Pg 139]

That the committee be asked to allow the General Secretary to write to every employer in the parish and district covered by the branch asking if they would consent to a rise of 1s. per week and to so arrange their hours of work as to enable their working week to finish at one o'clock on Saturday, and to make arrangements for this to commence on Saturday May 28th.

On this resolution being passed the committee withdrew to consider it. We discussed it most seriously, and I expressed an opinion to the committee that I considered the matter of such a serious nature that I thought the whole committee ought to be called together and decide the matter as a whole. Mr. Day did not think so, and reminded me of the resolution that was passed by the committee on April 25th on the motion of Mr. Winfrey, M.P., which absolutely prohibited me calling the committee together for such a purpose. My other two colleagues agreed, and they passed the following resolution:—

That the request of St. Faith's Branch be granted and the General Secretary be instructed to write to every employer in the district as requested by the resolution passed by the branch.

They also decided that another special meeting of the branch and the Emergency Committee should be called for May 20th to receive the reply of the employers.

On returning to the room I informed the meeting of the decision of the committee. This was received with the greatest enthusiasm, but I left with a heavy heart as I could not see the end of it. I could see the beginning, but it is one thing to commence a strike and another thing to end it. I was, however, determined that I would do everything that was humanly possible to prevent a strike of this magnitude. I was also determined that so far as I was concerned the other officials and the Executive should take their share of the responsibility of what might happen, and that I would so frame the[Pg 140] men's request to the employers that it would open every avenue for a peaceful settlement and, if trouble did arise, that the whole fault should rest with the employers. I can't explain it, but I always had, from the moment I took a leading part in the Trade Union movement, the greatest horror of a strike, and would go almost any length to prevent it, so much so that many of my friends used to say that I went too far in my peace-loving methods. But I don't think I did, and in looking back over my long public life I don't regret any action I took in this direction. I have made many mistakes, but that is not one of them. When, however, I had to fight, I gave no quarter to anyone and fought with the greatest determination.

I had no time on the Saturday or Sunday to do any correspondence. On Saturday I had my County Council work to attend to, and on my return home I had my week's accounts to make up with my assistant, and on the Sunday I attended to my religious work, for I never neglected that for anything. But on the 16th inst. I wrote the following letter to the employers on behalf of the men:—

Dear Sir,

I am directed by the men in your employ who are members of the Labourers' Union to ask if you will consent to raise your men 1s. per week. Further, if you would be willing to so arrange the hours of work as to make it possible for their working week to finish at one o'clock on Saturday. They would also be glad if this arrangement could be made in time to commence on Saturday May 28th. I would be glad to receive a reply from you at the earliest possible moment.

Trusting that you will be willing to accede to the men's request, and, further, we would be glad to meet a number of the employers and discuss this matter and come to some reasonable arrangement, and thus prevent any dispute arising between you and your men with all the suffering and inconvenience that must inevitably follow.

Yours faithfully,
(Signed) George Edwards,
General Secretary.

[Pg 141]

I also wrote to the President of the Union, Mr. George Nicholls, M.P., also to Mr. Winfrey, M.P., the Treasurer, telling them I was sure some very serious trouble was taking place and that, although Mr. Day did not think so, I was strongly of opinion that the whole Executive ought to meet and deal with the matter at once. Unfortunately, Mr. Nicholls was not at home and the letter did not reach him in time to reply before May 20th. Mr. Winfrey after a day or two did reply and said he thought we on the spot could deal with the matter, and there was no doubt we should have to support the men. I received no reply from the employers.

On May 20th the special meeting of the branch was held at the King's Head, St. Faith's. The large club room was packed to overflowing. Unfortunately, only Mr. Day and myself turned up. My other two colleagues did not attend. Mr. George E. Hewitt again presided, and I reported that I had received no reply from the employers. The men at once became indignant at what they termed a great insult to them. I saw at once that all hopes for peace were over. I could not but confess that the employers had treated the men with scant courtesy. A very angry discussion arose and in the end the following resolution was passed:—

That we ask the committee for permission to give the employers a week's notice, and that, unless our demands are granted, we shall cease work on Friday.

Mr. Day and myself retired, and I again told him that I felt very strongly that the whole committee ought to be called together, as I felt this was too big a responsibility for us. He again objected and said I must not call the committee together, especially after the Treasurer had written and said the committee did not want to meet. I therefore decided to face the situation bravely, and we went back into the meeting and informed them we had decided to give them permission to hand their[Pg 142] notices in. I then addressed the men and urged upon them to enter into this contest thoughtfully and seriously. Their claims were just and reasonable, and I was sure if they acted soberly and orderly they would have the public with them.

The question then arose as to what form the notice should take. I advised them to draw up what is known as a round robin and each man sign it. This was done and a notice was drawn up for each employer. It read thus:—

We the undersigned workmen of yours hereby give you notice that unless we receive 1s. per week rise of wage upon our present ordinary rate of wage on next pay day, also an agreement come to whereby our hours of labour be so arranged that our working week finish at one o'clock on Saturday, this notice will terminate on Friday May 28th.

Each man signed it and a notice was handed in to each employer on the Saturday morning May 21st. The employers received the notice as far as I could learn without comment and very little was said during the week. I at once took steps to grapple with the situation. I got a strike committee formed and got proper pay-sheets printed, which every man would be asked to sign at nine o'clock every morning at the club house. At the same time I intended to explore every avenue during the next few days before the final crash came to secure peace. On Monday morning May 23rd I received the following letter from Mr. J. T. Willis, Secretary of the Farmers' Federation.

Sheringham,
May 22, 1910.

Dear Sir,

On behalf of the farmers of the neighbourhood of St. Faith's, to whom you wrote on the 16th inst., I am directed to reply that they very much regret they are unable to accede to either of the men's applications contained in your letter to them. They quite appreciate the suffering and inconvenience and bad[Pg 143] feeling which is the inevitable result of a strike and would do everything to avoid one. It is not a question of paying the farm labourers as little as 13s. or 14s. per week, for it is well known that the average earnings inclusive of piecework pay amount to a considerably higher figure. During the past winter farm hands in the St. Faith's district received wages on the scale that had been paid during the summer instead of being dropped during the days of short hours as is usual. The farmers in that district recognized that circumstances then justified their paying what in fact amounted to an increase of 1s. per week wage. If instead of adopting this plan they had followed the usual course of dropping the wages during the period of short hours in the winter and had now raised their men to 13s. per week, probably there would now have been no discontent and they would have saved money. The result of the farmers paying higher wages during the winter than was from their point of view necessary, as labour was not scarce, is that they are now confronted with a demand for further increase for which the price of farm produce affords no justification. As you are probably aware, the market value of wheat is about one-third less than it was a year ago, and this reduction is not counterbalanced by better prices for other farm produce. The employers regret to hear that many of their workmen who have been in their service the greater part of their lifetime are intending to sever such old associations, perhaps against their personal inclination.

However, in case the threatened strike should be carried out, steps are being taken to fill the vacancies which will be so caused.

Yours faithfully,
(Signed) J. T. Willis,
Secretary.

George Edwards, Esq., C.C.,
Gresham.

To this I wrote the following reply, to which the Secretary of the Farmers' Federation never replied:—

Gresham,
May 25, 1910.

Dear Sir,

Yours of the 23rd to hand re the labourers' dispute at St. Faith's, and I very much regret to see by it the employers are not prepared to meet the men on either of their requests. I had hoped, considering the serious consequences involved both to the employers and employed, the employers would have been willing to meet the men and endeavour to come to some agreement without a strike having to be resorted to. I wish also to say my[Pg 144] Executive entirely disagree with your Executive that the present state of agriculture does not guarantee any advance in wages on the present wage.

We are of opinion, considering the much higher price they have to pay for their food and that the purchasing value of their wages is greatly depreciated, that they are entitled to some little advance further. We consider that, had the employers reduced wages last autumn, they would have treated the men most unjustly, and, further, my Executive thinks the threat thrown out in the last paragraph of your letter, namely to fill up the men's places, does not manifest a very conciliatory spirit. If the employers had first shown a willingness to meet the men in some way, it would have been much better. We hope, however, the employers and your Executive will yet consider their decision and meet us with a view to preventing a strike with all its bitter consequences.

Yours faithfully,
(Signed) George Edwards.

J. T. Willis, Esq.,
  Secretary, Farmers' Federation,
  Sheringham.

The receipt of Mr. Willis's letter, if I had any hopes that a strike could be avoided, would have dashed all hopes to the ground. Still I was anxious to catch at the last straw and to prevent a strike if possible. Also, when the history came to be written, it should never be said that I was the cause of it and that I did nothing to prevent it, for I did everything that any man could do to bring about peace. And in this story of my connection with the Trade Union movement I very much regret to say that, until the late Great War, the farmers never would meet the men nor their representatives, but persisted in dealing with the men in a most highhanded autocratic manner. Had they shown any kind of a conciliatory spirit nine strikes out of ten that have taken place during these last fifty years would have been avoided.

On Friday May 28th the notices handed in by the men expired, and, as no attempt on the part of employers had been made to arrive at a settlement, the men brought[Pg 145] their tools away. I cycled over from the other side of Norfolk where I had been holding meetings during the week. Also my assistant, Mr. Thomas Thacker, was present. On arriving at the village we found the greatest excitement prevailing. We were met by the men and their wives, also a number of Trade Union friends from Norwich. Amongst them was Mr. W. R. Smith, Mr. W. Holmes and Mrs. Reeve. Mr. Day was also present. A meeting was held under the tree that stood on an open space close by the King's Head Inn. Almost the entire village was present. Stirring addresses were delivered by the Norwich friends. Representatives of the press were present, and in order that the public might know that I had made every effort to prevent trouble, I read a copy of the letter I had sent to the employers at first, also the letter I had received from Mr. Willis, the Secretary of the Farmers' Federation, and my reply to it. It was generally admitted that I had gone the full length any leader of a Trade Union could go in the direction of peace. In fact some thought I had gone a little too far, but I felt, and I do now, that it is better to err on the side of peace than it is on the other side. But the fight had begun and I felt the whole brunt of it would fall on me. I therefore set my teeth and made up my mind that, as my efforts for peace had failed, I would fight like grim death and, if we were to suffer defeat, the fault should not be mine. Altogether I had 105 men on my hands, 75 at St. Faith's and 30 in the Trunch district. The Norwich friends offered to render as much help as possible and undertook to have collections made at all the factory gates on Saturdays to raise a fund to pay the men who were married and with families more than strike pay. I also decided to make collections throughout the Union. I also decided to hold big Sunday demonstrations throughout Norfolk and to make collections. The meeting concluded about ten o'clock, and I went home with my friend Mr. George Hewitt to stay[Pg 146] for the night, but not to sleep, for there was no rest for me. The responsibility was too great for me to rest, and I wished I could have had an Executive that would take some share of it. But I had a good lot of local workers. My friend George Hewitt, the branch secretary, undertook to act as strike secretary and to see the men sign the day-sheets. The next morning the village was full of excitement. At nine o'clock a number of mounted police arrived in the village and an equal number of foot police, for what purpose no one ever knew. I, however, saw the danger. Before leaving for Norwich I summoned the men with their wives to the branch house and warned them to be on their guard and give every instruction to the pickets to keep strictly within the law of peaceful picketing, and not on any account to attempt to molest the non-unionists when they were at their work, only to use peaceful persuasion on the road and in every respect to carry the fight on in an orderly manner and not in any way to run contrary to the authorities, for I was satisfied they would receive the greatest provocation. This they assured me they would do, and I am pleased to say, in spite of what was said to the contrary, that the men through the eight months' struggle acted in the most orderly way and only in the most technical manner did they overstep the bounds of the law.

On Friday June 4th I received the men's first lock-out pay from the Treasurer. On Sunday June 6th I arranged for a big demonstration at Weasenham, which was addressed by Messrs R. Winfrey, H. A. Day, R. Green, James Coe and myself. A collection was taken at both meetings for the lock-out fund amounting to over £7. The meetings were attended by over 1,500 people. An Executive Emergency Committee meeting was held after the afternoon meeting. Mr. H. A. Day presided, and there were present Mr. Winfrey, Mr. Robert Green and myself as General Secretary. It was resolved that the men out on strike at St. Faith's be supported according to[Pg 147] the minute passed at the Executive Meeting held on April 25th, which read as follows:—

Any member having paid three months' contributions and his entrance fee be paid full lock-out pay, but the General Secretary shall deduct from his first week's lock-out pay three months' contributions to bring them into compliance with Rule 6. But members having paid less than three months' contributions shall receive grants on the following scale: Married men, 7s. 6d. per week; single men, 5s. per week.

Mr. Winfrey also offered at this meeting to find work on the co-partnership farm at Walpole for sixteen men, the General Secretary to pay their rail fare. On Monday June 27th I took sixteen men over to Walpole. Arrangements were made for the men to have all their food in the Jepson Hall and that building to be used as a living room for the men. I purchased earthenware and cooking utensils for their use. One of the men was elected to act as cook and to keep the place clean. A good building at the farm was cleaned out and made fit for the men to sleep in and good clean straw was put into clean bags for beds. Each man took some bedclothes for himself, and thus I got them settled and saw them at work next morning before leaving.

The Norwich friends did splendidly. Our men stood at the factory gates on Saturday. The boxes were never opened without us finding from £12 to £20, and with the collections at our Sunday meetings I was able to pay married men 2s. per week above their lock-out pay and 1s. per head for each child, both in the St. Faith's and Trunch districts. I always paid the men at St. Faith's on Friday and the men at Trunch on Saturday. Never once was I an hour late. The men at St. Faith's always cycled on the road to meet me and act as my bodyguard, for the farmers' tools had again become threatening. Although we had nearly cleared the farms, there were then, as there always have been, some to do the bidding of the opponents of Labour; but the men in both districts[Pg 148] took very good care no one should harm me. These two disputes created great interest in the Union. My assistant Mr. Thomas Thacker and myself held meetings during the week, opening branches almost everywhere, and the Union went up by leaps and bounds. The labourers joined every week in hundreds, and, had the Executive let me have another organizer or two and more clerical assistance at home, the strikes would not have affected the funds of the Union to any great extent. The dispute, however, though serious and causing me many anxious moments, was not devoid of its humorous side. I always stayed with my friend Mr. Hewitt on Friday nights, and after the men were paid I always held a meeting under the tree which is now an historic one. The whole village would turn out to these meetings; the women were most enthusiastic. They were always on the look out for the blacklegs, as they would call them, and if one did venture to come anywhere near the village he would have to undergo some good-natured chaff. The employers were careful not to let these come too near the danger zone.

The Federation had provided very comfortable huts for them to live in on the farms and, when they had to pass through the village, they conveyed them in carts guarded by policemen. There was no necessity for that, and it was a wicked waste of time and money for which the county had to pay. The men and their wives had received instructions from me that they were not on any account to molest the strike-breakers, however great the provocation, and they loyally carried it out, for no leader of Labour in time of disputes ever had more loyal followers than I had in the St. Faith's and Trunch districts. But I could not always be with them, as I had to stump the county holding meetings in the interest of the Union, and the young folks and the women would have a little harmless horse-play. But the employers grew more bitter every day and apparently were determined to compel[Pg 149] these poor people to break the law. Writing twelve years after this dispute I can write more calmly and yet more deliberately, and I assert without fear of contradiction that there was a deliberate attempt on the part of someone to compel these poor people in some way to lay themselves open to be prosecuted, and that the authorities were anxious to embrace the first opportunity to punish severely these poor people for daring to demand the right to live by their labour and to see their wives and children properly fed and clothed.

One day the occasion arose, although no one could ever say that there was any attempt to molest the strike-breakers or in any way to use violence towards them. When these men were being conveyed from one farm to another guarded by the police about twelve of the men's wives gathered together with kettles and saucepans and sang one of the Union's songs on the approach of the blacklegs, and, although they never approached nearer than one hundred yards to the strike-breakers, they certainly followed them through the village, beating their tin kettles and singing their Union ditties. They were summoned by the police and appeared before the magistrates at the Shirehouse, Norwich. They were ably defended by our solicitor, Mr. Keefe. Although he proved that there was no breach of the law of intimidation, the magistrates bound these women over to keep the peace for six months. But soon another occasion arose for these people to be cruelly persecuted. One of the men, after urging upon his fellow workers to strike, had gone back again to work. One afternoon he went to work on his allotment. About twelve of the men went to the allotment gate with tin kettles and a concertina and waited until he came out to the road to go home, and without saying a word to him walked about one hundred yards behind him, playing their concertina and singing one of Sankey's hymns, "Kind words can never die." The wife, hearing the singing, came out into[Pg 150] the road and began to shriek out and make a dreadful noise and shout out, "Oh, they will kill my husband!" although no one was within a hundred yards of him, nor did they intend to be. But this was enough. The men were summoned by the police to appear before the magistrates at the Shirehouse, Norwich, on August 20th. Mr. Keefe was instructed to defend the men. I was unable to attend the court as I had to attend to two other emergency committees in connection with the harvest disputes. But Mr. Herbert Day, the Vice-President, was present in the court on behalf of the Union, and, although the police were unable to bring one solitary witness forward to swear that they saw anyone touch the old man or even go near him, the magistrates decided to convict and fined the men £5 each with costs.

The total amount was £60 16s. or three months in prison. Mr. Herbert A Day at once wrote out a cheque for the amount and prevented the men from going to prison. This money he paid out of his own pocket and never took a penny from the Union, and, further, for months in addition to what the Union, paid the men with families he gave the married men with families 1s. per child. The report of the conviction, when it appeared in the daily papers on August 22nd, caused widespread consternation and indignation at such a sentence being passed on poor helpless men. Never before since the scandalous sentence of seven years' transportation passed on the Dorchester labourers on March 15, 1834, by Judge Baron John William, the prosecution that was ordered by Viscount Melbourne, the Whig Home Secretary who was out to crush the rising spirit of Trade Unionism, had there been such outspoken criticism of any magistrates' sentences, nor had there been such a spirit of indignation. On every Labour platform throughout the country the sentence was denounced as being most unjust and cruel, and, instead of it in any way damping the spirit of the labourers, it created a widespread interest, and[Pg 151] through the efforts of my assistant I was able to report up to September 30th that we had enrolled into the Union in Norfolk over 1,800 members. Many expressions of gratitude were given to Mr. Day for his great spirit of humanity and kindness. But many of the leading Trade Unionists thought it would have been best to have let the men go to prison and to have taken steps at once to get the conviction quashed, which they said we should have had no trouble in doing, as it would have been the means of bringing even a more widespread sympathy to the men and to our cause.

During the summer months a great deal of controversy took place in the press, and I as a rule came in for a great deal of personal abuse and was accused of making the gulf wider and wider between employer and employed for no other motive than my own personal interest. Well, those that made that charge and heaped that abuse upon me would not have said so if they had had to work night and day as I had for 23s. per week and to bear the responsibility of a dispute with a hundred men involved and an organization so rapidly growing in strength and influence. But on July 3rd and 4th I embraced the opportunity of again making known to the public that I was anxious to do anything that any human being could do without giving away absolutely the men's case, which I knew was just and reasonable. There appeared in the Daily Press the first week in July a letter from Mr. J. H. Bugden suggesting that a conference should be held between the two sides with an independent chairman with a view of arriving at a settlement that would be honourable to both sides concerned. On going over to St. Faith's on the Friday to pay the men I addressed a meeting and said that I had seen in the press during the week a good deal of correspondence concerning the dispute in the St. Faith's and Trunch districts, and I was very pleased to see a letter from the pen of my friend Mr. J. H. Bugden suggesting a conference between the[Pg 152] two sides concerned, with a view of bringing this unhappy dispute to an end, and I wished to let it be known publicly that we were quite as willing and always had been to enter into negotiations with the employers or the Executive of their Federation with a view of bringing this dispute to an end, but up to the present they had declined all such offers that I had made and now we would go a step further. If such a conference could be held, we would accept Mr. Bugden as chairman. On July 6th I wrote from Castleacre to the Secretary of the Farmers' Federation the following letter:—

Castleacre,
July 5, 1910.

J. T. Willis, Esq.,
   Secretary, Farmers' Federation,
Sheringham.

Dear Sir,

As I stated in my speech on Friday last at St. Faith's, in replying to the correspondence in the Daily Press, we are quite willing to enter into negotiations with the Executive of your Federation re the dispute in the St. Faith's and Trunch districts, and would quite willingly accept Mr. J. H. Bugden as chairman of a conference, and, in case the parties not agreeing or not being able to come to terms, we would be willing to submit the whole case to an arbitrator, to be named and appointed by the joint members of the organizations assembled. Or, if the employers in each affected district prefer it, we would be willing to have an equal number of the employers and an equal number of the employees with the Secretaries of the Federation and the Labourers' Union to be members of the conference to represent the two organizations. Each labourer to meet without prejudice. Of course, if your Executive and the employers fall in with this suggestion other preliminaries can easily be arranged. An early reply would greatly oblige,

Yours faithfully,
(Signed) George Edwards.

P.S.—If you reply to-morrow, Wednesday, please direct your letter to the address below,

Visiting Committee Board Room, County Asylum,
Thorpe, Norwich.

[Pg 153]

I ought to say I was absolutely unable to get my Executive together to discuss the dispute further before the regular quarterly meeting, which was not until July 30th. I wrote this letter entirely on my own responsibility, irrespective of what they might say in reference to my action, but I felt the responsibility too great to let an opportunity pass that might bring peace.

On July 9th I received the following reply from the Secretary of the Farmers' Federation:—

Sheringham,
July 9, 1910.

Dear Sir,

I placed your letter of the 5th inst. before the Executive Council of the Farmers' Federation at their meeting to-day, and they regret they are unable to see that any good would result from a conference with representatives of the Labourers' Union. The Farmers' Federation has no dispute with the Labourers' Union, the present trouble being one between five or six employers and their labourers. All that the Farmers' Federation is doing is to assist its members in resisting the demands made upon them by the labourers who were in their employ.

Yours faithfully,
(Signed) J. T. Willis.

George Edwards, Esq.,
Secretary,
Eastern Counties Agricultural Labourers'
and Small Holders' Union.

To that letter I sent the following reply:—

Gresham,
July 11, 1910.

J. T. Willis, Esq.,
Secretary, Farmers' Federation,
Sheringham.

Dear Sir,

Yours of the 9th inst. to hand, and I very much regret that the Executive Council of the Farmers' Federation could not see their way to accept the offer of this Union to meet in conference with a view of bringing about a settlement of the St. Faith's and Trunch districts disputes. It must be obvious to[Pg 154] them, as they are supporting their members in the dispute, that they are an interested party in the dispute in just the same way as the Labourers' Union is by giving support to its members. It would have been a wise and humane policy for the two organizations to meet and endeavour to bring about a settlement. We having made the offer and not for the first time, and the Federation have refused it, now the onus must rest on the Farmers' Federation, whatever may be the evils arising out of their refusal. There would have been no lowering of the prestige of either of the societies had they met in conference. But your Executive seems to ignore entirely the last paragraph in my letter where I offered on behalf of the men for an equal number of the men to meet an equal number of the employers and only the secretaries of the two organizations to attend the conference of the employers and their men. By your making no mention of this part of my letter I take it that that offer is rejected too. Such being the case, there the question must rest so far as we are concerned, and we must leave the public to judge which side has acted in the most conciliatory spirit.

    Yours faithfully,
    (Signed) George Edwards.

This ended all efforts for a settlement so far as I was concerned. All future efforts would have to be left to others. If the men had to go down then I would go down with them, but I would go down fighting. I ought to say also that Sir Ailwyn Fellowes, now Lord Ailwyn, expressed a willingness to intervene if both parties agreed. I at once on behalf of the men agreed, but the Farmers' Federation refused. And so the dispute continued and, as the weeks went by, the relationship became more strained. I think I can say never was there a Labour dispute when so many efforts at securing a settlement were made by the men's leaders as I made on this occasion, and never a leader's efforts thwarted by the employers' organizations as mine were by the Farmers' Federation. It seemed that they could not bring themselves to see that the days of autocratic methods of dealing with their men were fast passing away and that the days of collective bargaining were rapidly approaching. They constantly kept the old parrot cry, "I always did do as I liked with[Pg 155] my men, why can't I now?" Happily there is a better spirit existing now. Both sides do meet together now and discuss these problems, but it is a sad reflection that it took a great war to bring about this long-desired change.

[Pg 156]

CHAPTER XIII
DEFEAT

The committee at their quarterly meeting held at Cozens' Temperance Hotel, at King's Lynn, on Saturday, July 30th, decided, on the motion of Mr. Winfrey, to move the office of the Union from Gresham to Fakenham, if a suitable house could be found, and they appointed Mr. Robert Green and myself a sub-committee to secure one if possible. This we did after a good deal of correspondence. We first agreed on one on a seven years' lease in Walsall Terrace, Queen's Road, Fakenham, at a rental of £17 per annum and rates; but before the agreement could be signed and the lease drawn up, it transpired that the house was let to another man without the knowledge of the house agent. Then a Mr. Philips of Fakenham offered us Wensum House at Hempton, near Fakenham, at a rental of £20 per annum. This we accepted and took on a seven years' lease. This was a ten-roomed house with two large attics. The two front rooms were very large. One of the front rooms was taken as an office, and it was a very fine and suitable room at that time, and quite large enough to be used as a board room for the committee. The committee also decided that I should pay them the same rent as I paid my landlord for my cottage and garden at Gresham, namely £5 per year. The moving from my village caused me a good deal of pain, but I knew I must bow to the inevitable, for the Union had outgrown my little bedroom. I did, however, love my garden and my little cottage, small as it was.[Pg 157] I cultivated my garden as a relief early in the morning when at home to occupy my mind from the worries of my official duties. I always managed so that I had some kind of vegetable all the year round. I was very fond of vegetable marrow and used to grow a very fine kind. We ate some as vegetables, the rest we could cut and keep and my wife would make what we called in our agricultural labourer's phrase, "million pies."

83

My wife, too, was very fond of fowls, and we kept just enough to produce a few eggs for our own use. To my little cottage my dear wife and myself were devoted. In fact, I was as proud of it as any duke is of his palace. We had two downstair rooms, the front room 12 ft. by 14 ft., its height about 6 ft. 8 in., the back kitchen which we used to live in most of our time 9 ft. by 7 ft. There was a little cooking-stove in it and a perpetual oven in the wall in which my wife did most of her baking. The front room floor she covered with cocoanut matting and put a nice paper on the walls, and there were plenty of pictures and my bookshelf at one corner full of books, of which I am so proud. As we both looked at this little cottage home, which had so many sweet memories, one can understand how unwilling we were to leave it. Further, I was living there amongst my own fellow agricultural labourers, and the environments and surroundings were so dear to me as to be part of myself.

THE FIRST OFFICE OF THE AGRICULTURAL WORKERS' UNION, GRESHAM, NORFOLK.
THE FIRST OFFICE OF THE AGRICULTURAL WORKERS' UNION, GRESHAM, NORFOLK.

I was also Superintendent of the Primitive Methodist Sunday-school, Society Steward and Circuit Steward of the Sheringham and Holt Primitive Methodist Circuit. To take me from it all was a wrench indeed, and I don't believe my dear wife ever did settle down to the change.

In moving into a town and a bigger house I knew I should be lifted out of my natural environment, which was no small matter now that I had reached sixty years of age. Besides, I was moving many miles from the spot which was so sacred to me, namely the village churchyard of Aylmerton, where I had buried my aged mother some[Pg 158] eleven years before. But the movement that I had so successfully launched and for whose success or failure I was responsible I felt had a greater claim than any other earthly consideration, so I braced myself up to the inevitable. Those memories of the past are still, however, sweet to me, and, if I had my choice, I think I would prefer to go back to them again. On October 11, 1910, I moved from Gresham to Wensum House, Hempton, near Fakenham, with all unforeseen events to face which I think I have done bravely.

But during all my moving troubles I had still the strike troubles to bear and the propaganda work of the Union, and no extra help allowed. My assistant Mr. Thomas Thacker had resigned in August through ill health, and his successor, Mr. James Coe, could not take up his duties until after harvest. No sooner had I settled down in my new office, nicely fitted up, than I saw I had great troubles to face which would cause me greater worries than ever I had been called upon to bear, for the strike continued as fiercely as ever, and I could see a crisis coming which I knew would be either the making or the undoing of the Union. At the conclusion of the harvest in the third week in September I met all the men on strike in both districts who had lost their harvest through the strike and paid them the whole harvest wages which they would have received had they been at work. So no one man suffered the loss of one penny through the strike. Such a thing no Union had ever done before.

During the quarter from July to October we had some few little disputes over the harvest wages, at Swanton, Morley and Litcham, in which Mr. Arnett, a member of the Executive, and myself were able to effect a satisfactory settlement. On November 19, 1910, a most important meeting of the Executive was held at Cozens' Temperance Hotel. There were present Mr. George Nicholls, Mr. Richard Winfrey, Messrs. George Edwards, J. Arnett,[Pg 159] T. Giles, A. Gidney, W. Codling, A. Petch and J. Stibbons. I presented my financial statement and quarterly report, which read as follows:—

In presenting you with my fifteenth quarterly report I am sorry to report for the first time a considerable decrease in our accumulated capital due to the prolonged dispute in the St. Faith's and Trunch districts. We have enrolled during the quarter 1,048 members. Our contributions have been £348 17s. 8d., which is £82 13s. more than the previous quarter and is the highest on record. We have held during the quarter fourteen camp meetings, which were all well attended. The collections taken have been devoted to paying the expenses of the meeting, and the balances have been given to a special lock-out fund for men with large families.

The dispute at St. Faith's and Trunch still continues at a very heavy cost. We paid to the men from June 30th to September 30th at St. Faith's £683 14s. 9d., Trunch £9 5s., Swanton Morley £9, Litcham £3 0s. 5d., Castleacre 10s., Pulham 5s. Total amount of strike pay during the quarter £705 15s. 2d., a sum for such a purpose we must all deeply regret. We can, however, congratulate ourselves on the fact that we have done more for our members in the time we have been in existence than any other labour union has ever done in so short a time. I feel, however, that we must now consider the next step to take. The St. Faith's strike has entered upon its twenty-sixth week. I have done all I can to bring the dispute to a peaceful and honourable conclusion, but have failed. The St. Faith's strike is costing £35 per week. I have appealed to the Board of Trade and clearly pointed out the miserably low wages paid to the agricultural labourers in Norfolk, and asked the President of the Board to intervene. He has, however, refused to do so. The next step I should advise the committee to take is to ask the members to express their views by ballot and at the same time point out to them the seriousness of the situation. Great care, however, must be taken in the matter, or we shall lose a great deal of the ground we have gained. The special effect the strike has had on the Union in Norfolk is that it has prevented the farmers reducing the labourers' wages from 13s. to 12s. per week during the autumn. We have appeared to the farmers to be a great deal stronger than we really are. And I do not consider the money we have spent in the dispute has been spent in vain and, further, it has created a lively interest in the Union. I wish to point out that the trouble at Litcham and Swanton Morley would have taken a very serious turn had it not have been for the firm stand your Emergency[Pg 160] Committee took. The dispute at Trunch still continues, but several of the men have found work with other employers. There is some little trouble arisen in one of our branches over a very difficult matter. The branch asks the Executive to support the case. Another little trouble has arisen at Felthorpe, which after very close investigation I am supporting, and I ask for your endorsement. In closing my report I wish to say we have received enormous support from our Norwich friends, both morally and financially, and great thanks are due to them from the committee. I feel I ought not to close this report without mentioning the fact that Mr. Herbert Day, our Vice-President, has been untiring in helping the men out on strike. He nobly came forward when they were shamefully persecuted and fined a sum amounting to £68 16s. and paid this himself. I hope the criticism and the discussion on this report and the position of the Union will enable us to come out of this crisis successfully. I also wish to report that I attended the Trade Union Congress held at Sheffield in September and moved the following resolution as instructed by the General Council:—

"That it be an instruction to the Parliamentary Committee to take steps to get the agricultural labourers included in the Trades Board Act of 1909."

The committee endorsed my report. Mr. Arnett also reported that he had received some communications from Mr. Leadbeater, a schoolmaster at St. Faith's, offering to negotiate with the farmers with a view to bringing the dispute to an end if the Executive wished.

It was resolved that Mr. Arnett be empowered to ask Mr. Leadbeater to negotiate with the employers at St. Faith's with a view to their taking the men back at 13s. per week, the wage which the men struck against.

To this I strongly objected, contending that the committee had no right to authorize anyone to negotiate with the employers on such terms until the members of the Union had given them the power to do so. I at once found I was up against my Executive. I also could plainly see that the Union was about to pass through a most severe crisis, and without great care the movement for which I had worked so hard for the last four years would be smashed. The committee also decided that a ballot of[Pg 161] the members should be taken and the resolution should be sent to all the branches. It was also resolved that as soon as I received the ballot papers from the branches, if the majority were in favour of the resolution, I should at once inform Mr. Arnett of the result, and that I should instruct Mr. Arnett to ask Mr. Leadbeater to make arrangement with the employers to take the men back on the old terms, namely 13s. per week and the hours of labour as before. Thus it will be seen all through nothing was in the circular about the terms. The committee decided without even meeting to discuss the ballot that the strike was to be closed and the men sent back on the old terms. As I look back at this proceeding I am not surprised that there was serious trouble, but I am surprised that the whole movement did not collapse. I am sorry to have to recount this, but I feel in writing my life-story and of the whole facts of the progress of this movement which I founded and the vicissitudes through which it had to pass, the whole facts should be made known. Further, most of it is a matter of history now.

The resolution and ballot the committee themselves drew up and instructed the President and myself to sign. This read as follows:—

To the Secretary of the..............Branch.

Most Urgent.

Sir,

Please call a special meeting of your branch not later than Saturday November 26th to consider the strike at St. Faith's. The Members of that branch last May asked their employers for 1s. per week rise and for their working week to finish at one o'clock on

Saturdays, which was equal to shortening their hours of labour three hours per week. The employers refused to grant either of these requests. A strike ensued which has lasted just on six months and has cost the Union over £900, which your committee consider a most serious matter. We had hoped the dispute would have been brought to a peaceful and honourable settlement. We consider the time has now come when you ought to have the seriousness of the situation placed before you,[Pg 162] for you to decide by your vote whether the committee shall not try to bring the dispute to an honourable conclusion. You must call a special and urgent meeting and put the following resolution to the meeting, sending us the result. Please write the number of votes for and against on your ballot paper signed on behalf of the committee.

(Signed) George Nicholls, President.
George Edwards, Secretary.

Resolution.

That in the opinion of this Branch the Executive Committee of this Union should immediately take steps to bring the St. Faith's strike to an honourable conclusion.

Number of votes.
For
Against
———

I received the ballot papers back from all of the branches by November 29th. On counting them, I at once sent the result to Mr. Arnett as instructed by the committee. The result was as follows for closing the strike as per resolution:—

For 1,558
Against 802
———

Majority for closing 756

Mr. Arnett on receiving the result at once wrote to Mr. Leadbeater and received the following letters:—

St. Faith's, Norwich.
December 3, 1910.

Dear Mr. Arnett,

I had a long interview with Mr. W. W. Cook last night, and with slight reservations he is willing to take the men back again at the old rate of wages. We discussed matters very fully, and finally I think Mr. Cook is prepared to deal very fairly with the men. Of course there will be certain sore places for a time, but he will not be vindictive. The modus operandi of closing[Pg 163] the strike will require great care. The Federation men will have to be cleared away in a proper way and our own men will have to be prepared to take their places at the most convenient time. This will require delicate handling, and I hope any statement made before the matter is closed will be well guarded. I sincerely hope you will be able to bring the issue to a satisfactory conclusion. I believe this is a chance, and in any way I can help you I hope you will let me know and I will gladly assist. Kindest regards,

>Sincerely yours,
>(Signed) H. Leadbeater.

St. Faith's,
December 5, 1910.

Dear Arnett,

Mr. Cook suggested yesterday that I should write to Mr. Willis, the Federation Secretary, and give him an account of Friday's interview. I am doing so by this post. I think this is a step nearer and may lead to an official recognition and discussion. Mr. Cook also told me yesterday that he was prepared to take on the evening school lads at once, if I send them in to him. What do you say to this? Let me know as soon as you can and then some start can be made. Hoping for the best, believe me to be acting in your best interest,

>Yours faithfully,
>(Signed) H. Leadbeater.

St. Faith's,
December 13, 1910.

Dear Arnett,

I have received an answer from Mr. Willis, the Federation Secretary, in which he informs me that the local masters will treat with their employees in a most friendly spirit and will at once employ them at the same rate as before. This is from the Executive Council, and I, knowing the feeling of our best farmers, beg to suggest that all pressure should be made to settle the matter at once. I feel sure, if the chance goes by, there will not be another on such good terms as now. This is the climax, and under no consideration will the men receive better terms. I should say if once acted upon there will be practically very few left outside. I think it is far better to keep the two or three left on the Union funds than to keep on a hopeless fight. Believe me, it is a hopeless fight, and I hope for the sake of the Union and the men the end has come and that your Executive can see[Pg 164] it. Kindly let me know what your Executive say so that I can report finally the result of my endeavours to bring about a settlement which will give us peace.

With my good wishes,

>Yours sincerely,
>(Signed) H. Leadbeater.

This was the first stage of the trouble. On receiving these communications from Mr. Arnett I at once summoned the Executive together, and they met on December 17th. A strange thing happened at the committee held on November 19th. Although the committee decided to take this course, they suspended me and my assistant organizer Mr. James Coe for a period during the General Election, and left only my secretary in the office to attend to all correspondence and keep the books. Of course I had to do all correspondence which had all to be sent on to me.

The Executive Committee met at the office of the Union on December 17, 1910, and there were present Mr. H. A. Day (Vice-President), who presided in the absence of the President, Messrs. A. Petch, W. Codling, J. Stibbons, M. Berry, J. Arnett, G. Edwards and T. Thacker.

It soon became evident that the committee would be hopelessly divided on the St. Faith's dispute. I reported the result of the ballot and that I had carried out the instructions given me at the last committee meeting, namely I had sent the result of the ballot on to Mr. Arnett and that I had instructed him to ask Mr. Leadbeater to make arrangements with the employers for the men to go back on the old terms of 13s. per week and the working hours to be as before. I had, therefore, carried out all my instructions in reference to the matter. Mr. Arnett was asked to state what he had done in the matter, and he then read the correspondence he had had with Mr. Leadbeater, and he strongly recommended that the arrangements made by Mr. Leadbeater with the[Pg 165] employers be carried out and that the men be instructed to return to work on the employers' terms. Mr. Day then moved and Mr. Berry seconded that the General Secretary be instructed to write and thank Mr. Leadbeater for his kind efforts to bring about a settlement of the St. Faith's strike, but, as the employers had not given any guarantee that they would take all the men back without any further reductions, the present negotiations be brought to an end.

This resolution caused a most heated debate, and there voted for it Mr. Day, W. Colding and Mr. Berry, against Messrs. Arnett, Petch and Stibbons. The chairman gave his casting vote for the resolution and it was adopted.

The Secretary read a letter from the St. Faith's Branch containing a resolution passed by that branch:—

That this branch is of opinion that the resolution sent by the Executive to the branches to vote upon was rather misleading. We ask the Executive to take another clearer ballot of all the members. If the strike shall continue for 14s. per week or go back for 13s. per week, if the employers will give an undertaking to take all the men and lads back at one time, and that a clear financial statement be given with the ballot. Further we are prepared to loyally abide by the wishes of our fellow members.

Mr. Day then moved and Mr. Berry seconded that another ballot be taken of all the members and that they be asked to vote on the following questions:—

1. Shall the men stand out for 14s. per week?

2. Or shall they go back for 13s. per week if all the men and lads are taken back at once?

Further, that the following circulars be sent with ballot papers:—

To the Secretary of the............Branch.

Most Urgent! St. Faith's Dispute.

Seeing that the words "honourable conclusion" in the first ballot were not clearly understood, we ask you to call another[Pg 166] meeting and take a vote of all your members present and let me have the ballot papers back not later than January 1, 1911. I am also instructed to let you know the true position of the Union. We report to you that since the strike commenced at St. Faith's last May we have enrolled nearly 2,000 members. We had in hand on September 30th last over £1,100. Since then we have spent £500 for strikes and general purposes and received about £250, so that we now have about £850 in hand. At this rate of expenditure and income we could continue the strike for another six months certain, that is until next May. We understand that the farmers have often trouble with the imported strike-breakers. The men at St. Faith's are prepared loyally to follow the wishes of their fellow Trade Unionists and either continue to stand out for the 14s. or go back for the 13s., if all can be taken back together. If the vote is in favour of the men going back for the 13s., then the General Secretary be instructed to act on the other resolution.

Signed on behalf of the committee,

Geo. Edwards,
General Secretary.

This was carried by the casting vote of the chairman. At the conclusion of the meeting I at once had this circular printed. It was finished that evening and I sat up all night and addressed the copies ready for post the next Sunday, as I had a religious service to conduct on Sunday. I would not neglect my religious work for anything. The committee also decided by a majority in which I voted that unless guarantees were given by the employers to the satisfaction of the General Secretary and the Union's solicitor, Mr. W. E. Keefe, the strike was to continue.

These decisions of the committee were, however, not allowed to remain unchallenged, for I at once received instructions from the President, Mr. George Nicholls, to call a special meeting of the Executive, which I did for December 28th, and there were present Messrs. George Nicholls, R. Winfrey, George Edwards, J. Arnett, T. Giles, A. P. Petch, J. Stibbons, M. Berry, W. Godling and T. Thacker.

The committee discussed the strike at St. Faith's. The strangest part of the proceeding is that although[Pg 167] they had confirmed the minutes of the last meeting without rescinding anything, they at once set about taking steps to ignore what was done at the Executive held on December 17th.

Mr. J. Arnett at once moved, seconded by Mr. J. Stibbons, that Mr. George Nicholls and Mr. Richard Winfrey be instructed to visit St. Faith's and use their endeavours to bring the dispute to a close on the honourable terms mentioned in the first ballot papers and that they have full power to act. Before this was put I pointed out that by the instructions of the meeting held on December 17th I had sent out fresh ballot papers which were not all returned. Further, they had just confirmed what that meeting had done. But they persisted in putting it to the vote, and Messrs. G. Nicholls, R. Winfrey, A.

P. Petch, R. Green, J. Arnett and J. Stibbons voted for it. Against it were Messrs. H. A. Day, W. Godling, M. Berry and myself.

After the meeting Mr. Nicholls and Mr. Winfrey proceeded to St. Faith's and interviewed Mr. W. W. Cook and the other employers and came to the following agreement: The employers undertook to take back at once thirty-three out of the seventy-five now on strike at the old rate of wages, viz. 13s. per week and the hours of labour as before. This arrangement left forty-two men for us to support. This was communicated to me, and I at once summoned another meeting of the Executive on Wednesday January 4, 1911. All the committee, with the exception of Mr. Thacker, were present. Mr. Winfrey at once moved and Mr. Stibbons seconded that the seventy-five men now on strike at St. Faith's receive full strike pay up to Friday January 6th, and that the thirty-three men who the employers have agreed to take back be instructed to see their employers and proceed to work on Monday January 9th, and that strike pay be continued to the remainder for the present, and that the committee meet again on January 28th to consider[Pg 168] the matter further. Mr. Day moved and Mr. Codling seconded an amendment that a third ballot paper be sent out, stating that Messrs. Nicholls and Winfrey had visited St. Faith's and find that the employers were only willing to take back thirty-three of their employees and that forty-two men would not be taken back. Some might be taken back by degrees. The members should be asked to vote on these points:—

(1) Shall we accept the employers' terms?

(2) Or shall the strike continue and a levy of 1d. per member per week be made to enable the men to be paid without further loss to the Union?

Before the question was put I pointed out to the committee that I had received the result of the second ballot, and I did not see how they could ignore that, for it would be an insult to the members, which I was sure they would deeply resent, and further, how could they accept such terms as the employers offered, when not only were the employers exacting their own terms, but they were not willing to take back more than 40 per cent. of their men? Such a settlement was unheard of in the history of Trades Unionism.

In spite of this the question was put, and there voted for the amendment Messrs. H. A. Day, W. Codling, M. Berry and myself.

For the resolution Messrs. G. Nicholls, R. Winfrey, J. Arnett, T. Giles, A. P. Petch and J. Stibbons. The resolution was carried and I was instructed to take steps to carry this out. I then gave the result of the second ballot:—

| For continuing the strike | 1,102 |
| Against continuing the strike | 1,053 |

Majority for standing out   49

Thus the strike that had lasted nearly eight months was brought to a close, not because the funds of the Union[Pg 169] were exhausted, but because the majority of the committee honestly believed that it was to the interest of the men and the Union that it should be closed.

I and those of the committee who were in the minority thought it was a grave mistake, and I think so to-day.

The troubles of the Union, however, were only just beginning.

Mr. Day wrote to the press condemning the action of the committee and publicly advised the members to take the matter into their own hands by demanding a General Council Meeting as per Rule 3, Section 3. This brought to me scores of telegrams and letters demanding that I should call a General Meeting to undo what the Executive had done. Of the many letters I received the following is a specimen, and shows the feeling that existed amongst the members on the whole matter:—

Kenninghall,
January 6, 1911.

Dear Mr. Edwards,

I have read in the press with deep regret of the way in which the committee have stopped the St. Faith's strike. If it is true that the farmers at St. Faith's have said, and I have it from good authority, that they were prepared to give the 1s. per week, but did not like giving the three hours on the Saturday, in the face of this how is it they were willing to send the men back without even asking for the 1s. or even a promise that it should be given on a certain date or when the men could work the full hours? And, further, they are sending the men back against the express wish of the whole Union. I certainly thought the funds of the Union belonged to the members and that they had power to say how their money should be spent and not the E.C.

I strongly protest against the last two committee meetings being called at all. The first one was called before the second ballot had come in and when it was in the hands of the members to decide. The second one was called after the members had decided how their money was to be spent and the committee went and reversed what the members had decided. I say emphatically the Union never ought to have been saddled with the expense of either of these two. The expense ought to have fallen on those who called the E.C. together. No doubt we shall hear[Pg 170] at the General Council that we ought to cut down expenses. I can see no reason, if half a dozen men can spend our money in that fashion, why we should not call a General Council to deal with the whole question as far as our members are concerned. They strongly protest against the entire action of the Executive in regard to the St. Faith's strike.

Yours truly,
(Signed) J. Sage.

I received many more letters much more strongly worded, giving the names and number of members who wanted a Council to be called. Eight branches sent in requests for a Council. The Executive met again on January 12th, when I placed in front of them the telegrams and letters I had received demanding that the Executive Committee should call a General Council to discuss the closing of the St. Faith's strike. By a majority of the Executive they decided, on the motion of Mr. Winfrey, that Rule 3, Section 3, stipulating that the E.C. shall summon a meeting of the Council on a requisition signed by not less than fifty members representing five branches, had not been complied with.

The whole question of the St. Faith's dispute was adjourned until the General Council meet on February 25th. At this meeting it was evident that the committee were hopelessly divided and that quite a party spirit was being manifested. I also became conscious of the fact that there would be a most bitter attack made on Mr. Day and myself at the General Council meeting by the Treasurer of the Union on the St. Faith's dispute. But I was determined that as far as I was concerned I would carry out every instruction the committee had given me. On Friday January 6th I went over to St. Faith's and paid the men out on strike and reported what I had already informed them by letter, the conditions of settlement, namely that the employers had agreed to set to work thirty-three of the men out on strike at the rate of 13s. per week and the working hours the same as before,[Pg 171] and that these thirty-three men were to present themselves at their employers' ready for work on Monday morning January 9th. I also informed them that the Executive would continue to support those left out until they met again, when the whole situation would be revised. The men received the information with tears, as they felt the whole case was given away, and I don't think I ever spoke with greater emotion, to see these brave sons of the soil after so many months of battle go back on the same terms as they had left, and what was worse they were compelled to go back and leave forty-two of their fellow workers still out. That was worse to them than going back. They felt that was a sacrifice too great to make and those that had stood by them were to be the first to be victimized.

My old friend George Hewitt, the branch secretary, was specially marked out for victimization. No one would employ him at any price. I gave the men as much encouragement as possible by assuring them that the Union would not let them starve. I told them they had fought a noble battle, and although they apparently had suffered a defeat in their first engagement, still the day would come when their efforts would be crowned with victory if they would but stand firm. This seemed to give them a little courage, and we concluded the meeting by singing one of our Union songs that we had sung many a time during the campaign, to the tune of "Lead, Kindly Light."

1. Strong human love, within whose steadfast will
Is always peace;
O stay with me storm-tossed on waves of ill,
Let passions cease.
2. The days are gone when far and wide my will
Drove one astray,
Which leads thro' mist and rocks to truth and good.
Be with me, Love, thou fount of fortitude.
[Pg 172]
3. Whate'er of pain the passing years allot
I gladly bear;
With thee I triumph whatsoe'er my lot
Nor can despair.
Freedom from storm thou hast immortal song,
Peace from the fierce oppression of all wrong.
4. So may I far away, when night shall fall

On light and love,
Rejoicing hear the quiet solemn call
All life must prove.
Wounded, yet healed, by Man beloved forgiven.
And sure that goodness is my only heaven.

As we sung it the old club room resounded again and again, and the sobs of the women were heard above all. But a note of sadness was sounded at the thought that they had not won. It was a time of inspiration to me, and I had a stronger faith than ever that right would yet triumph over wrong. I advised the men to be loyal to the decision of the Executive and present themselves at their various employers' on the Monday and to show no spirit of bitterness to those non-unionists they would have to work with. This they promised they would do. I also promised those who would be left out that I would come over each week and pay them. My old friend George Hewitt, though he was going to be one of the scapegoats, did not lose heart, but braced his companions up and told them to be of good cheer.

[Pg 173]

CHAPTER XIV
PARTING FROM OLD FRIENDS

As the time drew near for the General Council to meet there was every evidence that the meeting would be a stormy one. Resolutions for agenda condemning the Executive for closing the St. Faith's strike came in by the score. Letters of protest poured into the office. I drew up my report, got the books audited, got the balance sheet printed ready for the meeting as instructed by the Executive, prepared the agenda, hired the Town Hall and Assembly Rooms at Fakenham for the day and invited the representative of the press as ordered by the Executive. I also prepared myself for the attack that I knew was going to be made on me. The Executive met at the office of the Union. The Executive dealt one more blow at the St. Faith's men by carrying a motion that all strike pay cease after a week. Five voted for it and four against. The meeting was stormy all through.

On the Saturday morning my assistant Miss Pike and myself were up early and got everything ready for the meeting. Every delegate was presented with a balance sheet and a copy of my report as he came into the hall. Exactly at 10.30 a.m. Mr. George Nicholls took the chair; on his left sat Mr. Winfrey, the Treasurer. I sat on his right, and the following were on the platform: Messrs. T. Giles, J. A. Arnett, J. Stibbons, A. P. Petch and M. Berry. Mr. Godling was at the door as steward.

After the roll call was taken and the minutes of the last meeting read and confirmed, my report was taken[Pg 174] and discussed, at the suggestion of the chairman, before we proceeded with the election of the officers. The following is a summary of it:—

Fellow Workers,—In presenting you with my fifth report I wish again to thank you for the confidence you have placed in me during the year; also all the kind friends that have rendered me such valuable help during the year. The year has been a most eventful one. Great interest has been taken in the Union. We have enrolled over 2,000 members since I last gave my report. In May last the men in St. Faith's and Trunch districts got restless. The men at St. Faith's put in a demand to the employers for 1s. rise and their working week to finish at 2 p.m. on Saturday. This was refused and the men came out on strike on May 28th and have been out on strike ever since. The committee on December 28th decided to close down the strike at St. Faith's in consequence of the financial strain.

At the conclusion the President gave his address in which he rather severely criticized the strike and said had he been at the committee meeting he should not have sanctioned the men coming out on strike on such a request.

Mr. Winfrey condemned the strike and accused Mr. Day and myself of sanctioning the strike without consulting the rest of the committee, and said he did not know anything about it until he went to Weasenham on June 6th, after the men had been out on strike a week. I replied to this rather warmly, pointing out that I carried out to the very letter the resolution he (Mr. Winfrey) had moved at a committee meeting held on April 25th, and, further, that I received a cheque from Mr. Winfrey on June 4th to pay the men their first lock-out pay—so how could he say he did not know? Further, before the strike commenced I had written both to the President and the Treasurer begging them to let me call the committee together to discuss the whole situation.

The discussion was carried on during the day with great spirit and incriminations were indulged in from all sides.

[Pg 175]

A motion of censure on the Executive was moved by Mr. G. E. Hewitt on behalf of the St. Faith's Branch for closing the strike. This was as follows:—

That this Council protests against the dishonourable way the Executive closed down the St. Faith's strike.

After a long discussion the resolution was put to the meeting and carried by a large majority.

The President, Mr. Geo. Nicholls, at once handed in his resignation, and although he was unanimously requested several times to withdraw it, he refused to do so. Mr. Winfrey refused to allow his name to go to the ballot for the treasureship. Mr. Day was opposing him. Mr. W. R. Smith was elected president by a large majority. Mr. W. B. Harris vice-president, Mr. H. A. Day treasurer, and the following were elected to serve on the Executive: Messrs. J. Arnett, W. Smith, G. E. Hewitt, W. Holmes, R. Green, H. Harvey, W. G. Godling, M. Berry and James Coe.

Mr. Nicholls then left the chair, and he with Mr. Winfrey retired from the meeting. Mr. W. B. Harris occupied it for the rest of the business, but the meeting was too excited to transact much business and it ended in confusion. Thus ended the first chapter of the Union.

I left the meeting greatly perplexed, wondering if the child I had brought into being was going to be killed in its infancy. I knew its life was in terrible danger, having passed through a similar experience in the years that were past. I had, however, great hopes for the future.

I think that I ought not to close this stage of the Union's history without paying a tribute to those who were going out of the movement and who jointly with me had done their best to build up the Union to its present position. In the previous pages in giving the facts of the struggles we had to pass through in the early stages of the Union it might appear that I complain rather bitterly of my colleagues who had worked with me during[Pg 176] the four years, but nothing of the kind is my intention. No body of men have worked with greater honesty or were prepared to make greater sacrifices in the cause of human progress. Neither the president, Mr. Nicholls, nor Mr. Winfrey nor Mr. H. A. Day ever took a penny piece for time, rail fare or out-of-pocket expenses, and on one occasion these three gentlemen paid for the delegates' lunch at one of the General Council meetings. No member of the committee ever charged more than 2s. per day and his rail fare, and for the first twelve months took only their rail fare. In fact, in March we had a balance at the bank of £1,569 0s. 10d. saved in less than four years, and, when it is remembered that the members only paid 2d. per week contribution or 8d. per month, it must be admitted that there is great credit due to those men who had given so much time and labour to build up a movement of this kind. Most of them were inexperienced so far as Trade Unionism was concerned.

The only mistake they made was that they endeavoured to build a strong labourers' Union on strictly commercial lines, which was not humanly possible; but the mistake was a creditable one, and these pioneers of this movement will go down to history as having laid a foundation of one of the finest movements in the world's history. I can look back with my connection with these men in the early stages of this movement with the greatest pleasure. The work was hard but it was of the pleasantest kind, and although Sir Richard Winfrey, M.P., has since allied himself with a party that is anti-progressive, he has done some good work for the agricultural labourers. I am sorry we shall always have to remain in opposite camps, and I feel it my duty to appear on a platform in opposition to him, still he must be given credit for the good work he has done.

The same must be said of my friend Mr. George Nicholls. I only wish he had stayed with us. He could have done far more useful work, but this separation is only what[Pg 177] has always happened in times of strikes. I have never known a strike so far as agricultural labourers are concerned without it has either ended in a split or a large number of the labourers concerned leaving the Union, and that is one of the reasons all through my long connection with the Labour movement why I have always been against the strike weapon being used until every other means have failed to secure justice. Even a victory by a strike is dearly bought. I would commend this experience to my young readers who are coming along in the Labour movement in the future. For strikes in the future will be more dreadful than they have been in the past.

[Pg 178]

CHAPTER XV
THE NEW MODEL

The General Council being over and the new Executive being elected, they were called upon to bring to a close the strike according to the decision of the old Executive, which, though we soon found it to be a very difficult matter, we set about in a business-like manner. In our President, Mr. W. R. Smith, and Mr. Holmes we had two men who had had wide experience in settling such things; this made the task much more easy, and we closed the dispute without inflicting more hardship than we could possibly help. Apart from this nothing eventful happened during the year. I set myself to work to prevent the split taking wider dimensions than could be helped, and I soon found that I had got a most sympathetic Executive Committee which made my task very much easier. The General Council meeting was held at Fakenham on March 9, 1912. The President, Mr. W. R. Smith, presided. To show the progress we had made during the year and the task devolving upon us, I will give my report as I presented it to the General Council:—

Respected Brethren,—In presenting you with my Annual Report and Balance Sheet, I wish again to thank you for the continued confidence you have placed in me during the year; also to thank the officers and friends who have rendered me such valuable service in carrying on the work of the Union.

Our worthy president, Mr. W. R. Smith, J.P., has thrown his whole soul into the work and has attended a large number of meetings, has cycled hundreds of miles without fee or reward, and in business meetings has proved himself a most able president. Mr. H. A. Day, our treasurer, has rendered most able assistance in putting the affairs of the Union on a better financial basis, while Messrs. J. A. Arnett, R. Green, W. Holmes and other[Pg 179] members of the Executive have all done useful work. We have also had the assistance of Messrs. Reeves, George Roberts, M.P., George Lansbury, M.P., Keir Hardie, M.P., Noel Buxton, M.P., and Joseph Fell.

We commenced the year under a very dark cloud. Differences of opinion had arisen over the conclusion of the unfortunate strike at St. Faith's, and because of these differences some of our old friends left us. Others prophesied that the doom of the Union was cast. We had also been seriously handicapped by hostile criticism in some journals, while others had not given us the same publicity as hitherto.

One of the first things your Executive did on coming into office was to put the Union on to a thoroughly business-like footing. All monies are now banked in the Union's own banking account. All monies are now paid by cheque drawn by the treasurer, and an entirely new system of book-keeping has been adopted and every account receives a double entry.

The Executive on coming into office had to bring the dispute to a conclusion according to the decision of the late Executive, and this we found to be a most difficult task. It could not be done without causing a deal of heart-burning amongst many of the members affected, and we had also to deal with one or two clear cases of victimization which we were bound to take up. Yet, notwithstanding this serious crisis, we have been able to hold our own. We have admitted during the year 617 new members. Our organizers have cycled thousands of miles in attending meetings. Mr. Coe has attended 183 meetings in Norfolk, 14 in Oxfordshire, 13 in Kent, total 210, and has cycled 3,240 miles. Mr. Codling has held 242 meetings in Norfolk, has walked 202 miles, and cycled 2,840 miles. I have attended 153 meetings in Norfolk for the Union, 12 in Kent, 18 in

Oxfordshire, total number of meetings for the Union 183. In addition to these I have attended 83 meetings in connection with my duties as Guardian and County Councillor. I have attended altogether 266 meetings and have cycled 1,866 miles and have travelled by rail 1,563 miles. The total number of meetings held in Norfolk is 751 and in other counties 57, giving a grand total of 808. Early in the autumn we received urgent appeals to visit other counties, and the committee yielded to the requests. So we have for some weeks past been carrying on a campaign in Kent, Oxfordshire and Bedfordshire, and have been able to open several new branches in these counties. New branches have been formed in the following places: Aylsham, Larkfield, East Malling, West Mailing, Offham, Ivy Hatch, Wateringburgh, Roughton, Monchelsea, Barming, Wardington, Croughton, Chacombe Evenly, Clifton, Souldren, Chipping, Warden, Cople, Biggleswade and Morening. Sixteen[Pg 180] small branches have become defunct in Norfolk. We have held fifteen Sunday meetings during the summer months, which again proved a great success and were attended by several thousand people. Collections were made at each meeting to defray expenses and there is a small balance left. The committee had hoped to have a good balance left to form a benevolent fund to help needy cases. The collections, however, did not come up to those of last year and several of the meetings did not pay their way, but the committee have been able to deal with some few cases out of the fund.

We have been called upon again this year to place a large number of cases in our solicitor's hands, and these he has dealt with in a most able and successful way. In three cases he was able to effect a settlement which put into our members' pockets £256 12s. 6d. In other cases he has been successful, as his report will show. I think the Union ought to congratulate itself that it has such an able advocate and adviser as Mr. Keefe. The committee wishes me to press upon all our members that they must not in any case settle the matter themselves without the solicitor's instructions when once they have placed the matter into our hands.

Our Union was again this year represented at the Trade Union Congress held at Newcastle in September. The committee sent two delegates, Mr. James Coe and myself. We were treated with great respect by the delegates and much sympathy was expressed towards our class when we related the great difficulties and the hardships they have to endure. The Trades Board Act resolution was carried unanimously and the Parliamentary Committee has already taken action. I attended the deputation to the President of the Board of Trade on February 26th and pointed out to him that a labourer with a wife and children, when he had paid for rent, coal and clothing, had only just a little over ¾d. per meal, and therefore you as a class were receiving much below a living wage. The President of the Board of Trade, whilst admitting that you were underpaid, asked for the Government to have time to work the Act before any more trades were included.

The President of the Board of Trade did the Union the honour of appointing two of its organizers on the Advisory Committee of the Labour Exchange.

Our President also has a seat on the committee, and I think that as time goes on we may be able to do some good by preventing Labour Exchanges being used to import blackleg labour in time of disputes.

Brethren, in closing my report let me give you a note of warning. We are on the eve of a great social upheaval, the greatest the world has ever seen. It has already begun with the great labour unrest through the industrial world. It is a proof that the workers are determined that better conditions of labour shall[Pg 181] prevail. A commencement has also been made in Parliament with social legislation, such as Old Age Pensions and the Insurance Act. The latter will come into operation during the year, and for the first time in the history of this country the State has recognized that it owes a duty to its workpeople by insuring them against sickness. There is, however, a grave danger that the capitalist class will use every means in their power to saddle the entire cost of the Act upon the shoulders of the workers by a reduction in their wages and an increase in their cost of living and thus prevent the toiling masses from obtaining the benefits of the Act. Unless our class take a timely warning they will be helpless. The capitalist class will fight with all their force to delay the day of social emancipation, and it will require the united action of the workers to prevent the capitalist and privileged class from crushing noble efforts that are now being made for industrial freedom. Your Union has now been in existence for five years. Its progress has not been so rapid as some of us had hoped after the bitter experience of the rural workers during their disorganized state. We thought that long before now at least 90 per cent. of the labourers would have been organized. That a large amount of time and money would have to be spent we were well aware, and that a great deal of opposition would have to be encountered, but the cost of establishing the Union has been beyond the wildest dream of any of us. I think the time has come when some steps ought to be taken to obtain some financial help for organizing work, because, as is shown in the financial statement, the contributions of the members have gone down during the year in Norfolk, which means that there has been a decrease in members largely due to a number of young men leaving the country for other spheres of labour. Notwithstanding this there has been a good awakening in other counties, and there is now a prospect of the Union becoming a national movement, which is essential if we are to take our part in the social battle that is about to be fought.

Yours faithfully,

(Signed) George Edwards,
General Secretary.

Wensum House,
  Hempton, Fakenham,
    December 31, 1911.

The officers were all elected and the delegates were well pleased with the position of the Union after it had passed through such a terrible crisis. The breach that was made the year before was apparently healed and I was enabled to proceed with my work with a much lighter[Pg 182] spirit, as it was evident the Union would very soon leap forward during the year. The Executive had decided to become an Approved Society under the Insurance Act. I had been elected by the Government to serve on the Advisory Committee under the Act. I was also elected to serve on the Advisory Committee of the Labour Exchange. The work, however, at the office was becoming very much more complicated through the Union becoming an Approved Society, and the system of book-keeping required by the Government was of such a nature that my assistant, Miss Pike, felt she was not equal to it. I too was not up to book-keeping of that kind, for it required an experienced clerk, and the committee were compelled to dispense with the service of Miss Pike, greatly to my regret. Mr. R. B. Walker, of Banbury, applied for the post, and in

June was appointed assistant secretary. This appointment released me more for outside work and enabled me to give more attention to the organizing department, and we were very soon able to make rapid progress.

During the year 1911 it became evident to me that my dear wife was fast failing in health mentally as well as physically, and that her end was drawing near. Her condition caused me the greatest concern and I looked forward to the future with dismay. But at the commencement of the New Year 1912 she apparently took a sudden change for the better, especially mentally—in fact, she became her former self again. This sudden change blinded me to the real state of her health and I seemed to buoy myself up with the hope that she would be spared to me for some few years and that she would again be able to stand by my side. I was, however, not to be long deceived as to her true state, for by the beginning of April the disease took a serious turn for the worse, she took to her bed and her suffering was great. For three weeks I never left her day or night. I never took my clothes off, but watched by her side. In this hour of sorrow I had one comfort, that her intellect was as bright[Pg 183] as ever. She made requests that I should not leave her, and I never did, and took great care that her every wish should be gratified. The last Sunday she was alive she made a request that the Salvation Army band should be asked if they would come and play under her window, and the tunes she selected were "Lead, Kindly Light," and "Nearer my God to Thee." This request was at once granted, and on the Sunday afternoon the band came and played as requested. They never played more sweetly and it was thoroughly appreciated by my dear one. On Monday we saw that the end was drawing near. So great was her suffering that on Monday I begged of Dr. Fisher to try to do something to ease her pain, which he did, and she passed a peaceful night. Early on Tuesday morning the effects of the medicine were exhausted and she was again racked with pain. About seven o'clock I saw the end was come.

She raised herself up in bed and placed herself in my arms and breathed her last.

The last words she said were "Good-bye, dear boy, I am going."

Her birthday was on April 22nd, and she died on April 24th. I laid her to rest in Fakenham Cemetery. I have erected a stone at the grave to her memory and the following inscription is on it:—

In Loving Memory
of
Charlotte Edwards,
The beloved wife of George Edwards, C.C.
Who passed away April 24, 1912.
Aged 70 Years.

I loved her, yes, no tongue can tell
How much I loved her, and how well;
Christ loved her too, and thought it best
To take her home with Him to rest.

"Thy Will be done."

THE LATE MRS. GEORGE EDWARDS
THE LATE MRS. GEORGE EDWARDS.

[Pg 184]

Had she lived until June 21st of that year we should have been together for forty years. We shared our joys and bore our sorrows together. Hers had been a lonely life, but she made the sacrifice for the Cause in which she was as deeply interested as I was myself. This shows the noble spirit of the woman and endeared her the more to me. No one can tell the lonely life the wife of a public man has to live, but she never complained.

She was always anxious to help me, and if she thought I was in any way depressed and disappointed she would cheer me up with kind words and press me on with my work. In fact, our lives had become one. That made the blow the heavier. I felt I had lost part of myself. In any case I had lost a good helpmate, and a chair became vacant that could never again be filled.

When my wife was laid to rest, then the effects of the loss fell on me with full force. Three weeks of anxious watching and the twelve months thought and care I had with her and the worry of the crisis the Union was passing through had told upon me. This caused me to have a serious nervous breakdown, and I felt sure the day was not far distant when I should have to lay down the cares of a responsible official life. I had, however, a most sympathetic Executive who did all they could to help me, and with their help I pushed forward. The Union made rapid progress. We extended our borders. We had a pressing invitation to open up a campaign in Lancashire, and during the summer and winter I addressed several meetings and opened up several branches in Lancashire. By the end of the year we had several hundred members in that county, and I see by the report which I presented to the General Council meeting held at Fakenham on Saturday February 8, 1913, that we had made more progress than at any time since the Union was inaugurated and had saved £138 18s. 9½d. The Council meeting was a very successful one. I again set[Pg 185] to work with great earnestness, but with impaired health and broken spirit.

I devoted a deal of time to Lancashire during the first month of the year. The Trade Union Congress held at Newport, Mon., in September 1912 elected me on the Parliamentary Committee of the Trades Union Congress. That was the second time the agricultural labourers had had a seat on the Parliamentary Committee. Mr. Joseph Arch was the first representative. During the year 1913 we made rapid progress in Lancashire, but it soon became evident that we were in for some trouble in that county, and in consequence I had in the early spring to devote all my time to it. I soon found that the varying elements were prominent and that I had quite a different type of man to deal with to what I had in Norfolk. They were very near the great industrial centres and had caught some of their spirit. I did my best to keep them calm, took every course possible to get into touch with the farmers, and succeeded in getting one interview at which the Union was represented by the president and myself. We tried to effect a settlement but failed, and on June 20th the strike took place, continuing until July 8th. The men's demands were to cease work at 1 p.m. on Saturday, 6d. an hour overtime pay, and a minimum wage of 24s. per week and recognition of the Union. By the second day of the strike we had just 2,000 men out. The men, however, displayed great determination and solidity, and obtained a rise of 2s. per week, 6d. an hour overtime and the working week to cease at 2 p.m. on Saturday. This was the first time in the history of agricultural labourers that they had obtained a reduction in the hours of labour.

At the commencement of the dispute I issued an appeal to the various Trade Unions and other friends, and the response was magnificent. I received something like £788. Mr. Noel Buxton sent a cheque for £100, and through[Pg 186] this response we only had to spend about £500 of the Union's funds, although the strike and other expenses connected with it cost £1,250. At the conclusion of the strike my old complaint returned again worse than ever and my nervous breakdown was complete. I felt there was no other course open for me but to resign, for I could carry on no further, and the Union had developed so rapidly that it was now beyond me. I came therefore to the conclusion that it would be better for the movement for younger men to take control. I had succeeded in getting what I had been fighting to obtain for years, namely the Saturday half-holiday.

On my return home I placed my resignation in the hands of the Executive. They would not accept it at the time, but gave me a month's rest. But at the end of the month I had to give up all hope, and the committee accepted the resignation with deep regret and allowed me to do what organizing I felt able to do. I moved into a private house in Fakenham with my wife's niece, Mrs. Kernick, who on the death of my wife came to live with me and look after me. During the winter I picked up a bit and was able to do some organizing work.

In 1914 I was appointed by the Lord Chancellor a Justice of the Peace for the County of Norfolk.

I also took some meetings for the National Land Campaign Committee, ceasing to receive any salary from the Union at my own request. In August the Great War commenced. I, like most of the Labour leaders, felt it my duty to do what I could to help the nation in the hour of need. I believed then, and I believe still, that Germany was bent on obtaining a world-wide military domination; I felt it my duty to put the Nation's interest before any other consideration. Not that I believed in war, for war to me is a crime of the deepest dye against humanity.

The Burston School Strike is one of the most interesting[Pg 187] and peculiar disputes I have taken part in. Here was I compelled to take sides against one of the committee of the County Council of which I was a member during the latter part of 1913 and the beginning of 1914. The Burston School teachers, Mr. and Mrs. Higdon, for some reason had a difference with the Managers, and as I read the particulars I came to the belief that there was some other reason for the Managers' action.

An inquiry that was held on February 23 and 29, 1914, as to the charges that the Chairman of the Managers' brought against the teachers showed that they were of a trifling nature and never ought to have been brought. I also thought, and still think, the decision come to inflicted a punishment upon the teachers far more severe than the case deserved, even if the charges were true, which I did not believe, and to me their dismissal which took place on March 31, 1914, was a clear case of victimization and I felt it my duty to support them. Soon after their dismissal the children all struck and refused to attend the Council School. Summonses were issued against the parents for neglecting to send their children to school. A large meeting was held on the green on the Sunday after the parents were convicted at Diss, which was attended by nearly two thousand people, and a resolution of protest was passed requesting that a public inquiry be held. I attended and gave an address. The meeting was conducted on strictly religious lines, and I took for my text "Thou shalt not bear false witness against thy neighbour."

After this meeting and after seeing the devotion of the people to the teachers and having satisfied myself that the teachers and the parents of the children were fighting a just battle, I decided that I would do my best to champion their cause. I will say, as I look back at the fight I have made on their behalf, I am satisfied I never championed a more righteous cause during my long[Pg 188] public life. I was sure, however, at the commencement of the struggle that I should have to fight almost single-handed so far as the County Council was concerned, for I had at that time only one Labour colleague on the Council, and that was my esteemed friend Mr. W. B. Taylor.

I should like to say that I never have accused any of my colleagues on the Council or on the Education Committee of being actuated by any spirit of unfairness or with any spirit of political or religious prejudice.

I have always contended that they acted in what, in their judgment, were the best interests of the education of the children; but I have always contended, and do to-day, that they allowed themselves to be biassed by the political prejudice of one or two of the Managers, and that was what I set myself out to fight. My first effort on the Council was to move that the Education Committee be requested to hold a public inquiry. On this being put to the vote only my colleague and I voted for the motion. My next effort on the teachers' behalf was to move that the Education Committee be asked to reinstate the teachers for the period of the war, in order that peace and concord might prevail in the village. On this occasion I warned the Council that unless something in the direction of peace was done, the whole great Trade Union movement would take the matter up, and then they would probably have another school built. My warning, however, was unheeded and the resolution was lost. This time I received a little more support, and Mr. W. B. Taylor, Mr. Coe, Mr. Day and Mr. Pollard voted with me. This brought public sympathy to the teachers. Many of the Trade Union leaders took the matter up, a subscription list was opened, hundreds of pounds were subscribed, a new school was built, which is called the Burston Strike School, and it stands there as a monument of what the subscribers believed to be[Pg 189] a great fight for religious and political freedom. I have never regretted the part I took in this great fight. I am, however, satisfied that had the County Council taken my advice at the time most of this unpleasantness might have been avoided.

[Pg 190]

CHAPTER XVI
THE GREAT WAR

On August 4, 1914, the Great War commenced and, as stated, I came to the conclusion, like most of the other Labour leaders, that according to the information I had at my disposal we had no other alternative but to enter the war. I felt that it was a struggle for our very existence; further, that we were fighting to overcome one of the greatest curses to humanity, namely the wicked spirit of militarism. I therefore decided to put what appeared to me at the time the nation's interest before any other consideration. I spoke at a good many recruiting meetings in the early stages of the war. So far did I carry my patriotism that some of my friends began to be rather nervous about me for fear I should carry it too far, but they need not have been, for I never deviated one iota in my views on the Labour questions nor was there any fear that I should ever leave the cause to which I had devoted all my life. I took, however, the view that it would be the poor that would be the first to suffer, should we be defeated or should the enemy succeed in starving us, as the following letter I wrote to the women of the country will testify. It appeared in the Eastern Daily Press:—

To the working-women of Norfolk, the wives and mothers and sisters of our brave boys who are now so gallantly fighting for their country in France and Belgium and other parts of the world.

I feel constrained to make an appeal to you in the hour of our[Pg 191] national danger to consider seriously the gravity of the situation and what it would mean to this country, especially the working classes, should Germany and her confederates win this war. Everything that is dear in our English life will be destroyed; all our hopes for improvements in our national life will be blighted; the working classes will be thrown back into far worse conditions than they were one hundred years ago; all our liberties so hardly won for us by our forefathers will be lost.

I ask you to consider for one moment what has taken place in Belgian and French towns and villages. The homes of the poor have been destroyed by fire and sword. Old men and women have been murdered in cold blood, women and children outraged and killed, mothers separated from their children and wives from their husbands, not knowing whether they are dead or alive. What these poor people have suffered is a small thing in comparison to what would happen to us should our enemies ever reach these shores, and they will unless we are able to defeat and destroy the cruel and barbarous military power of Germany. Do you wish your daughters to be outraged, your children slaughtered? Would you like to see our veterans of industry murdered, our homes burnt and our towns made desolate? No, I know you would not. No women are more devoted to their homes and loving to their children than the women of Norfolk. The danger, however, is very great and it can only be prevented by everyone doing all that lies in their power to help the nation in the hour of distress. It is for the protection of our own hearths and homes that we are engaged in this terrible war, hence the great call on the manhood of this country. And now the time has arrived when the womanhood of the nation have to be appealed to, and I am making a patriotic appeal to you, the women of my own country, to come forward and help in the present crisis.

In making this appeal to you I am asking you to do a thing which I had hoped you would never have been asked to do again and which, I am thankful to say, the improved conditions of labour have made unnecessary. But the crisis is so great and the danger of losing all that is sacred and good in our national life is so pronounced, that I venture to make this appeal to you to offer your services in cultivating the land in order that as much food can be produced at home as possible. There will be a great deal of work to do in the spring, such as hoeing and weeding, getting the land fit for the turnip crops and many light jobs which hitherto have been done by men; and, as there is a great shortage of labour, we will see that fair wages shall be offered to you. One of the first essentials of life is food, and if this cannot be produced, then a great disaster is staring us in the face. To[Pg 192] prevent this our womenkind are called to help. I therefore appeal to you in the name of God, who made you free, and in the interest of your children to help in this hour of need.

Yours faithfully,
(Signed) George Edwards.

Fakenham,
   January 3, 1916.

At the passing of the Military Service Act and the setting up of Tribunals, I with my old friend George Hewitt was asked by the Union to represent Labour on the Norfolk Appeal Tribunal, which we did. On that Tribunal we watched very closely the interest of the class we were sent there to represent. It was, however, a most unpleasant task and one that I would never undertake again, should the occasion arise, which I hope never will. Before leaving this matter and the part I took in the war I would like to say that I am bitterly disappointed at the result of the war, and it has entirely altered my outlook on war and its causes and has confirmed in my mind more than ever the opinion that force is no remedy, and that, unless the nations disarm and men devote their great inventive and scientific powers in the direction of peace, civilized man will soon be utterly destroyed.

At the setting up of the Norfolk War Agricultural Committee Mr. G. E. Hewitt and myself were elected on it to represent Labour. We were enabled on this committee to do some very useful work. Our business was to insist that the land be properly cultivated, also to force the bringing back of land that had been laid down to grass to arable cultivation. We had also to look after the service men who were medically unfit for foreign service, and who were transferred to the land, and to insist that the farmers treated them fairly. Another useful opportunity presented itself for me to do some work for the people on the establishment of the Food Control Committee. I was elected a Labour representative on the Walsingham District Committee and was elected chairman, a position[Pg 193] I held until the committee finished its work. I think I can claim that, with the assistance of my colleagues, we did some most useful work and administered the Act fairly between all classes. We certainly did prevent a great deal of profiteering and enabled the people to obtain their food on much better terms than they otherwise would have done.

On the passing of the War Pension Act and the setting up of War Pension Committees, I was elected on the Norfolk County Committee. I was also elected on the Walsingham War Pension District Committee and was appointed its first chairman, which position I held until I was elected a Member of Parliament, when I resigned in consequence of being unable to attend its meetings. But I look back upon my work on this authority with the greatest satisfaction. It was a humane work and a labour of love. It is the greatest joy of my life to know that I have been able to do something for these poor widows and children who have been deprived of their bread-winners when they most needed them, and further, to know that I have been able to help the poor fellows who have had their health wrecked through serving their country. During my term of office on this committee my house was always open to receive these poor fellows who sought my aid. In fact all classes came to me for help and advice.

It became evident early in the spring of 1915 that the agricultural labourers were becoming very unsettled and justly so. The war commenced in August 1914, and with it the cost of living went up by leaps and bounds, but the labourers' wages never rose a penny piece. At last the labourers informed the officials of the Union that if we did not move in the matter they would take the whole question into their own hands. We appealed to the farmers to meet us in conference and discuss the question, but they refused to meet us, and at last we had no other alternative but to issue notices to the farmers[Pg 194] for our men to cease work. One Friday in March there were sent from our office 2,000 notices. The next day, when I was at Norwich attending a County Council meeting, I met Mr. Keith of Egmere, who was a member of the Council, and this question of notices was discussed, and we both expressed regret that it was necessary to take this course. Mr. Keith asked me if anything could be done and said that Mr. H. Overman of Weasenham would like me to meet about five of the largest farmers at the Royal Hotel that day in Norwich. I told him that was impossible as I had no official authority to do such a thing. The President of the Union was not in the city and I could not get into touch with him. I therefore dared not do such a thing on my own authority and, further, I could not think of attending such a conference alone even if I had authority to do so. A few minutes after I met Mr. H. Overman and he suggested that I should meet the farmers unofficially and talk the matter over and see if it would not be possible to do something to get an official conference called during the next week and if possible prevent a strike. This I agreed to do on condition that Mr. Herbert Day, Treasurer of the Union, attended with me, and with the distinct understanding that our meeting should be absolutely informal and there should be nothing said or done that would have the least appearance of being official. This was agreed to, and at 3 p.m. Mr. Day and myself met Mr. H. Overman, Mr. Keith, Mr. Lionel Rodwell, Colonel Groom and Lord Leicester, the Lord Lieutenant of the County. In the first part of the discussion the farmers complained bitterly of the action of the Union in issuing notices. I told them I was not there to discuss the rights or wrongs of the action of the Union in issuing notices, but to see if something could not be done to get the two sides together. But I would say this: the Farmers' Federation was responsible for what had happened, for the Executive of the Union had asked the Federation to meet us over and over again,[Pg 195] but they had refused to do so. We had, therefore, no other alternative but to take the course we did, for our men were determined they would have a readjustment of their wages. But if there was anything I could do, even at the eleventh hour, to get the two sides together at a conference I would do it. After this little straight talk the farmers saw the difficult position we were in and expressed the opinion that the attitude taken up by the Federation was wrong. I think I ought to say that none of the farmers present were members of the

Federation, but they were the largest farmers in the county and the most influential and were almost able to force the issue. They promised that if the Union's Executive would meet them they would undertake to see that, whatever agreement was arrived at, it was carried out. With this understanding I undertook to use my influence with the Executive to have such a conference held at Fakenham. On my return to Fakenham I informed the General Secretary of what had happened and asked him to get into touch with the President and obtain his views on the matter, which he did, and I think I ought to say that my action was rather severely criticized by some of the Executive.

But the President put his foot down and was determined that such a conference should be held. It was arranged to meet the above-named farmers, with Lord Leicester in the chair, and the following were appointed to meet them at the Crown Hotel on Thursday in that week: The President, Mr. W. R. Smith, the vice-president, Mr. George Edwards, the General Secretary, Mr. R. B. Walker, and Mr. G. E. Hewitt. Mr. Smith put our case in such a reasonable and forceful way that it was unanswerable and put in a claim for a 5s. per week increase, bringing the wages up to £1. On receiving our requests and after some little discussion the farmers retired, and after some few minutes they returned and made us the following offer. They would agree to recommend to[Pg 196] the farmers a rise of 3s. per week at once if we would undertake to withdraw our notices. We withdrew and discussed the farmers' offer, and after some few minutes' discussion agreed to accept the offer as a compromise, and undertook on our part to withdraw all our notices. At the same time we informed the farmers that we considered we were justly entitled to the 5s. per week rise, but for the sake of peace we accepted the compromise. To-day I rejoice that I was the means of bringing the two sides together and preventing a terrible dispute. It was also opening up a new chapter in the history of the Agricultural Industry, for here was collective bargaining, something that I had been working to obtain for over forty years. Ever since the Federation has met us every year and our readjustments have been made in a most friendly manner, and many differences which would have ended in bitter disputes have been avoided. I do not think either side would like to go back to the old individualistic system of bargaining. At least I hope not.

For years at our Annual General Council I had moved a resolution requesting the Government to bring the industry under the Trade Boards Act. I had also moved it at several Trades Union Congresses and had attended as a deputation with the Parliamentary Committee of the Trades Union Congress before the then President of the Board of Trade and put our case in favour of it, but with very little success. My friend Mr. Noel Buxton, who was then member for North Norfolk, had moved a resolution upon it in the House in 1916. The matter had become so pressing that the Government could not resist it any longer, and in the spring of that year Mr. Lloyd George announced in a speech that the Government intended to bring in a Bill to be called the Corn Production Act, which was to set up an Agricultural Wage Board. This Board was to fix wages from time to time that should enable the labourer to keep himself and family in such a[Pg 197] state of health as would enable him to be an efficient labourer. It also fixed the minimum wage at 25s. per week. The Bill was brought in early in the session of 1917, and in it was inserted a clause fixing the minimum wage at 25s. per week. This to us at the time appeared to be a most inadequate figure as the cost of living had increased beyond all bounds, and we decided to use every means within our power to get that figure struck out and 30s. put in its place. We appointed a deputation to lobby the members when the Bill was passing through its final stages to induce the members to vote for the 30s. I was one of the deputation and I did my best to persuade those members I got into touch with to vote for the 30s. But the Government had made up its mind to stand by the 25s. Hence on a division the 30s. was rejected and the Bill became law during the session of 1917. I was elected on the first Central Wage Board. I was one of the Government's nominees. The Board consisted of sixteen representatives of the workers, sixteen employers and seven appointed members who were to take an impartial view and decide the question when the two sides failed to agree on an equality of votes. Eight of the workers and eight of the farmers with the appointed members were appointed by the Government and approved by the Minister of Agriculture, and, as stated above, I was appointed by the Government. On our side were Messrs. W. R. Smith (National Agricultural Labourers' Union), R. B. Walker, G. E. Hewitt, T. G. Higdon, Robert Green and W. Holmes. For the Workers' Union there were Messrs. G. Dallas and John Beard. There was one woman on the workers' side. The Government appointed Messrs. George Nicholls, George Edwards, Denton Woodhead, Haman Porter, H. L. Lovell, with Messrs. Gaurd and Richardson from Wales. We had our first meeting in November 1917. Mr. W. R. Smith was elected leader for our side. Sir Ailwyn Fellowes, now Lord Ailwyn, was appointed chairman, and he soon endeared himself[Pg 198] to all sides, proving himself to be a most able and impartial chairman. The first business of the Board was to set up District Wage Committees. We first decided to set up one committee for each county. Then the Board left it for each side to select their own representatives, and for us it was a most difficult task as we had two Unions catering for one industry and there was a great spirit of rivalry existing between them, which created a bitter spirit between the two secretaries. This was greatly to be regretted and caused friction when there ought to have been harmony. We always, however, showed a united front in the Board Room. Then there was Mr. Denton Woodhead, who represented some independent Friendly Society. It took us some weeks to set up the committees, and we were into the New Year 1918 before the Board could settle down to its real work of dealing with the wages. In the meantime the men were getting very restless, especially in Norfolk, as the cost of living was going up by leaps and bounds, and I could see serious trouble looming in the near future unless the question was tackled at once. I begged of the Board to set the Norfolk Wages Committee up at once and let us get on with our work. This they did, and I was put on the Norfolk Committee, and at our first meeting was elected leader of the workers' side. We had nine on each side, and there were five appointed members. Our side consisted of myself, Messrs. S. Peel, J. Pightling, R. Wagg, Mrs. S. Kemp, Messrs. H. Harvey, R. Land, W. Skerry and J. Shickle. Mr. Russell Colman was appointed chairman. At our first meeting I moved that the wages should be raised to 30s. per week for a 54 hour week and that the working week end at one o'clock on Saturdays. This was rejected absolutely by the employers, and they moved an amendment that the wages should remain at 25s. per week and the working hours remain as before. We had a long discussion, and at last the employers' section asked for the question to stand adjourned for a week. We objected, but[Pg 199] the appointed members agreed, and the meeting was adjourned until the following Monday week, when we met again and had a long discussion. The appointed members suggested time after time that the two sides should meet and come to some agreement. The employers withdrew their amendment and moved another that the wages be raised to 27s. 6d. per week and that the working hours be 57 hours per week. This we absolutely refused to accept and would not move one inch. The appointed members retired and discussed the matter. After a time they sent for the leaders of each side and made a suggestion in the form of a compromise. They would be prepared to vote for 30s. for a 55½ hours' working week. The farmers refused the offer. I went back to my colleagues, and after some discussion we reluctantly agreed to accept the compromise, and on the appointed members returning to the room they put their suggestion to the vote. The employers voted against; we voted with the appointed members, and it was carried, and the recommendations were sent to the Central Board which met the same week. The Central Wage Board rejected the 55½ hours and adopted our first proposition, namely 54 hours as a working week, and that the week's work end on Saturday at 1 p.m., or that there be one six and a half-hour day a week, all that was worked over to be paid for as overtime. We also fixed the overtime pay at time and a quarter for six days and time and a half on Sundays. We also raised the pay of the horsemen and stockmen in proportion. The Wage Board issued their notices accordingly, but it was issued in such a way that it was open to a grave misunderstanding and was misunderstood. The men and some of the leaders thought it came into force at once and several disputes occurred. I, however, took an opposite view and contended that it did not come into force for a month. For this view I was severely criticized and was accused of joining hands with the farmers to defraud the men. So much was this statement spread abroad that[Pg 200] I felt bound to defend my honour and challenged my accusers to point to one solitary instance in which I had played the men false. It was evident I was right in the view I held, and if my advice had been taken, a good deal of friction would have been avoided and the men would have had their one o'clock several months earlier, for the Board at their next meeting, while confirming the order, postponed the one o'clock on Saturdays until three months after the war was over. However, the men got their one o'clock on Saturdays after hostilities ceased, an improvement I had been fighting for for nearly fifty years. I hope the men, now the Wages Boards are abolished, will not barter away an improvement in their working conditions. I also hope the farmers will act in a good spirit and cause no friction by trying to force the men back to old conditions.

[Pg 201]

CHAPTER XVII
THE LABOUR PARTY

The Union had decided, after taking a ballot of the members according to the Act of 1913, to take political action and to be affiliated to the Labour Party. I at once decided to be loyal to my Union. Early in 1918 I publicly announced that I intended to sever my connection with the Liberal Party and that henceforth my influence should be given to the political Labour Party. I had for some time been getting out of touch with the Liberal Party. In fact, I always was an advanced Radical and had hoped the party would have advanced in political thought. But I had now become convinced that there was no hope that the Liberal Party would ever advance in political thought sufficiently to meet the need of the growing aspirations of the new democracy. I had therefore no alternative but to separate myself from the party I had so long been associated with. The wrench, however, was great, for I could not separate myself from old associates lightly, especially when it was a party in which I had received my first political education. But it had to come. My political thought had outgrown the old political clothes I had worn so long. Early in the spring of 1922 the Executive of the Union decided that they would place candidates of their own in the field at the General Election whenever it should come. They decided, however, that this should be carried out in the most democratic way. Every branch of the

Union was asked to send in nominations. This having been done, the Executive[Pg 202] decided that they would send five names out of the nominations received. They also decided that they would put three candidates into the field, as the National Labour Party had promised to give £1,000 towards the election expenses of two candidates that would be run under our auspices. The candidates that went to the ballot were R. B. Walker, George Edwards, George Nicholls, Capt. E. N. Bennett and T. G. Higdon. Those successful were R. B. Walker, George Edwards, and George Nicholls, Mr. Higdon being the next highest. Mr. Walker was selected by the King's Lynn Divisional Labour Party to contest that Division, and I was asked to meet the newly formed South Norfolk Divisional Labour Party with a view to making a statement on the current topics of the day. In my speech I severely criticized the Government's war policy and claimed that the war could have been ended some months before and a great number of precious lives have been spared had they embraced the opportunity that presented itself and entered into negotiations. In fact, I advocated peace by negotiation as I considered the time was come when every effort should be made to stop this horrible slaughter. I declared my adhesion to the Labour Party's policy and stated that on social questions affecting the lives of the people I stood where I did before the war. I retired for a few minutes, and on being called into the room I was informed by the chairman, Mr. E. G. Gooch, that the delegates had unanimously decided to invite me to become their prospective candidate to contest the Division at the General Election. I thanked them for their kind invitation and accepted it. On the Monday a full report of my speech and my adoption appeared in the press. I was, however, to have showered on my head storms of abuse. The writer of current topics in the Eastern Daily Press was particularly severe, and other writers in the press in their anxiety to discredit me did not hesitate to stoop to misinterpret my words. While I deeply resented the misinterpretation of words[Pg 203] and claimed that the services I had rendered to my country during the war were sufficient answer to my critics and that I was anything but disloyal to my country, I also claimed that I had a right to hold my own views on what I thought was the best method of bringing this terrible conflict to an end. My opponents made as much political capital out of it as they could, but I was satisfied that I was right, if not for any other reason, for the sake of humanity. On November 20, 1918, at a special meeting of the South Norfolk Divisional Labour Party I was formally adopted as their candidate, and the following is a press report of my address.

Mr. Edwards, who was loudly cheered, said he asked the electors to keep before their minds not persons but principles. He somewhat regretted that Mr. Soames had withdrawn, because he was certain that however much they might differ, he was a perfect gentleman, and they would have carried through the contest in a way that would have been creditable to them. Whoever might be their opponents, so far as he was concerned, he intended to act in such a way, whatever the result, that he should not have to look back with any regrets to the contest. He would give his opponents credit for being honest in their intentions. If he was reviled he would not revile again, but if character was attacked he would be compelled to defend character and the position he took up. No one regretted more than the Labour Party that the election had been brought upon them. The Government, however, had determined to go to the country, and the Labour Party took up the gauntlet and would fight for the principles they held dear. The Government said they wanted a mandate. What greater mandate could they have than a united people behind them, and they had a united country to back them up in their peace terms. What was wanted was a just and permanent peace, with no vindictiveness, and the Labour Party held the view that there was no safeguard for a permanent peace except on the grounds laid down by President Wilson. The Labour Party was going in for a League of Nations, for such a league laid down on the President's principles would mean a permanent peace, and bring about universal brotherhood. They meant by a League of Nations a league which should consist of all the civilized nations of the world, and that there should be such international dealings with all questions which would prevent war in the future. (Hear, hear.) What he understood when the [Pg 204]President talked about a League of Nations and no boycott was that there should be no preferential tariffs, and that all the nations should be dealt with alike. He wished those who talked about boycotting the Germans and taxing their goods out of existence would think for a moment. Germany was too big a nation to be crushed, and the war had taught us German science and inventions were not dead. If it was attempted to crush her she would prepare for another war, and England and other nations would also have to prepare, and the past war would be nothing as compared to another war. They had to consider the best way to meet the difficulties which had to be met in this country, and one of the first things was reconstruction, and how to help the men who had been fighting for us. The Labour Party would not have the same treatment meted out to soldiers as was meted out after previous wars. They stood for the discharged soldier, the wounded and the maimed, and would see that they were kept in a condition worthy of the nation for which they had been fighting. (Hear, hear.) That would be done without the taint of charity or pauperism. (Hear, hear.) So far as he could see, the Government's scheme for discharged soldiers was free insurance, a month's furlough, and thirteen weeks' out of work pay if they could not obtain employment. The Labour Party demanded that they should be returned to civil life and kept out of the State until employment was found for them at Trade Union rate of wages. (Hear, hear.) They stood for the bringing into operation at once of the Home Rule Act, and to see that justice was done to all and injustice to no one. They asked for a living wage for all workers, and their class having made the sacrifice they had—and he did not say the other classes had not done their bit—was not going back to pre-war conditions. Touching upon agriculture, Mr. Edwards said the Labour Party were going in for a wage which would enable parents to raise up healthy children. The first function of the party when it came into power was to see that a long neglected class was lifted up above the poverty line on which it had for so long existed. Everything had to come from the land, and if the farmer was to pay a living wage agriculture must be so reorganized that he could do so. The first thing was the farmer must have security of tenure; this he had not had, and he had not been encouraged to get the best out of the land. (Hear, hear.) There must be security of tenure for the farmers, and although he was a Free Trader, he should be in favour of the clause of the Corn Production Act being strengthened so that the farmer could pay the wage which might be fixed from time to time. He did not suppose he should live to see it, but he wanted the land nationalized. (Cheers.) He, however, wanted to see the antiquated land laws repealed. Mr. Edwards[Pg 205] also touched upon the housing question, and remarked that if Governments could find money for war they could find money for houses. Proper medical attention must be put within the reach of the poorest, and the National Insurance Act must be radically altered, and there should be State paid medical attendants. (Hear, hear.) He also advocated better wages for teachers, who were the greatest moulders of character in the country.

The campaign commenced in all earnestness. Meetings were arranged throughout the constituency, but at this time no other candidate was in the field. Mr. Soames, the Liberal Member for the old South Norfolk Division, had informed the Liberal Party that he did not intend to seek re-election, and it appeared for some days that I was not going to have an opponent at all. But in due course the two political parties combined to find an opponent in the person of the Hon. W. H. Cozens-Hardy, son of the late Lord Cozens-Hardy, and a most honourable opponent he was. It soon became evident that, while the fight would be fierce, it would be fought on clean and honourable lines. We both decided that we would fight on principles alone, and that we ourselves would not indulge in personalities, nor would we allow any of our supporters to do so. This we both carried out to the very letter. On one occasion we occupied the same pitch. I spoke for ten minutes first and he spoke for the next ten minutes, which was the allotted time of the meeting, it being held at the factory gates at the dinner hour. This spirit was manifest right through the contest. On the nomination day we both met in the Returning Officer's room and had a very friendly chat and arranged if possible to lunch together on the day of the poll at Diss. This arrangement, however, I was unable to carry out, as my motor failed me on my way and made me late. There is one peculiar feature about this contest. My opponent was the eldest son of the man, Mr. Herbert Cozens-Hardy, for whom I had worked so strenuously in 1885 as a Liberal and whom I had helped to win.[Pg 206] For doing so I had lost my situation, been turned out of my house and, as stated before, had been compelled to travel twelve miles a day to work as an agricultural labourer.

During the contest I received valuable help from my honorary agent, Mr. Edwin G. Gooch of Wymondham, a well-known Norfolk journalist and now a Justice of the Peace, a member of the County Council and other public bodies and Hon. Secretary to the South Norfolk Divisional Labour Party, who undertook the agency without promise of any fee or reward. The women in Wymondham and the men rendered magnificent work. All the envelopes were addressed and the addresses folded voluntarily. The local men supplied the platform with speakers. I also had the assistance amongst other visitors of the Rev. F. Softly from Fakenham and the Rev. Starling, and amongst my most earnest local workers were Messrs. W. J. Byles, J. Long, A. H. Cunnell, H. T. Phoenix, A. V. Gooch, George Mayes and E. A. Beck. More than passing interest was attached to the support I received from the Earl of Kimberley. During the contest I made my home with Mrs. J. Long at Wymondham, who looked after me with great care. A few days before the election I issued my address as follows:—

Ladies and Gentlemen,

I am invited by the South Norfolk Divisional Labour Party to contest the Division at the coming General Election, and consider it my duty to accept the invitation in the interests of Labour and Progressive Thought.

My full address will shortly be in your hands. Meanwhile may I briefly state my policy?

I stand for a League of Nations and reconstruction on sound principles, without reverting to the old unjust social system of pre-war days; for a just and generous provision for the discharged soldiers and sailors and their dependents, apart from either charity or Poor Law; for the prompt carrying through of a comprehensive national measure of housing and a national system of education.

Full provision must be made for the reinstatement in civil[Pg 207] employment on demobilization at Trade Union rate of wages and complete security against unemployment of all civil war-workers about to be discharged, and those whom the dislocation of industry will throw out of work. There must be a complete fulfilment of the nation's pledges to Trade Unions.

The complete restoration of freedom of speech and political action, with protection against victimization. The immediate abolition of all forms of compulsory military service.

Adult suffrage and equal rights of voting for both sexes. The immediate establishment of the fullest measure of Home Rule for Ireland. Full national control of all means of transport, and the retention by the State of all coal and iron mines, and all the means of production, distribution and exchange.

The reorganization of agriculture and rural life in such a way as shall secure to the agricultural labourer a living wage that will lift him above the poverty line and the fear of penury and want, but if this is to be done agriculture must be so reorganized that it will secure to the farmer conditions that will enable him to meet it. I therefore favour first the strengthening of the clause in the Corn Production Act, and fixing the prices of his produce at a figure that will enable him to pay a living wage for his labour as fixed by the Wages Boards from time to time. I am also in favour of so controlling the price of his feeding stuffs, seeds, and raw material that will prevent the profiteer from taking advantage of his needs in carrying on his industry. If the land of this country is to be brought back into a proper state of cultivation and be made to produce all the food it is capable of, then the farmer must have absolute security of tenure. All antiquated land laws must be abolished. There must also be drastic reform in our Game Laws. There must be a drastic alteration in the Small Holding and Allotment Acts. The small holder must be able to get his holding on the same terms as the large farmer. I am in favour of credit banks and a short credit system to enable the holder and the farmer to pay ready money for their goods.

The cruel and antiquated Poor Law must be abolished. A pension should be given to the poor widow with a family. There must be such a revision of pension rates and ages for eligibility for old age pensions as would enable the recipients to live in decency and comfort. A proper and adequate medical treatment ought to be secured to the poor, which in my judgment could be best obtained by a State medical service.

I appeal for your support on the grounds of the long public service I have rendered to the people by my work on many public authorities, especially during the last four years. Should you do me the honour of returning me as your member I will continue[Pg 208] to work in this new sphere in the interests of the great toiling masses to which I belong, and in whose interests all the best years of my life have been given.

Yours faithfully,
George Edwards.

Wymondham,
   December 1918.

I had magnificent and most enthusiastic meetings all through the campaign and had little or no opposition. It was generally agreed that I had by far the best meetings. I had, however, the whole force of the two political parties against me, and some of the members of my own Church in the Division were my bitterest opponents. But in spite of the good reception I had an impression all through the campaign that I was fighting a losing battle. I did not, however, let anyone of my friends know what I thought of the matter, but braced them all up. The only person I related my thoughts to was my dear niece, who gave me all the encouragement she could and stood by my side. The election took place on December 4th, but we had to wait until December 28th before the votes were counted. Directly after the election my niece Mrs. Kernick and myself went back to our own little home at Fakenham and anxiously waited for the day of the count to arrive. When December 28th arrived we were up early in the morning and made preparations to leave for Norwich where the votes were to be counted. We left Fakenham by the 9.45 a.m. train and arrived at the Shirehouse just after the counting had commenced. The counting had not gone far before I realized that my fears all during the contest were fulfilled and that, although I had fought a good fight for the principles I held to be good, I had been badly beaten and that the combined forces of reaction were too much for me. At four o'clock the counting was finished and the result was as follows:—

W. H. Cozens-Hardy   11,755
G. Edwards 6,596
———
   Coalition majority   5,159
[Pg 209]

After the declaration of the poll my friends and I returned to Wymondham and made for the Fairland Hall, which was packed. The meeting was of such a character as had never been held there before within the memory of man. It was attended by the leaders of all political parties; the Rev. E. Russell was in the chair. On one side of him was the victorious candidate and on the other side of him was myself, the defeated candidate. A resolution of congratulation was moved to the member, which I supported. A resolution was moved and carried thanking both candidates and the leaders of both parties for the clean and friendly fight we had made, neither candidate ever having said an unkind word towards each other, and it was expressed by both sides that we had lifted the political life of South Norfolk on to a high level. Thus we finished, as we had commenced, in a most friendly spirit. That election of 1918 in South Norfolk will rank as the cleanest and purest political fight that was ever fought.

The meeting being over, I returned to my home at Fakenham, no one knowing but my niece the effect it had had on me. No one knew the strain it was upon me to attend that meeting, but I intended to be brave and manly. It had made its mark which was soon to make itself manifest. As soon as possible I sent the following letter of thanks to all my supporters and voluntary workers:—

Parliamentary Election, December 1918.

To the Labour Party Workers in South Norfolk.

Dear Sir or Madam,

I embrace this opportunity of thanking you for the valuable help you rendered me during the recent election.

No candidate ever had a band of more loyal supporters, and I trust your great devotion to the Party will be recompensed by victory in the days that are to come. The ideals for which we stand are of the highest, but the forces of reaction were too strong for us this time. The time will come, however, when democracy will assert itself and the principles of righteousness and truth, for which we stand, will yet triumph.

[Pg 210]

My one hope is that you will go forth with renewed vigour, organize your forces, exercise patience and sweet reasonableness. I hope to live to see South Norfolk go solid for Labour.

Again thanking you for your support, and with best wishes for the New Year,

I am,
Yours faithfully,
George Edwards.

7 Lichfield Street,
  Queen's Road, Fakenham,
    January 1919.

As days went by my life told its tale upon me. I tried to be brave. I even endeavoured to hide my trouble from my niece, but her keen eye and affection and deep sympathy for me detected it and she feared the worst. But no one knew my pain outside of my home. I had, however, one little brightness brought into my life in this time of sorrow. In December I received a notice from the Secretary of State that the Prime Minister had recommended me to the King for the distinction of the Grand Order of the British Empire, known as the O.B.E. On January 3rd I was gazetted as O.B.E., and my name appeared among the list of Honours. In due course I received a command from the Lord Chamberlain to appear at Buckingham Palace in February to receive the decoration at the hands of the King. My niece feared that I should not be able to stand the journey. I also had my doubts. I took her with me. Within a few hours, however, after I left the Palace I broke down. My strength would hold out no longer and I had to keep in bed at the hotel where I was staying for a few days. I was, however, determined to get to my own home and took the risk and travelled home to Fakenham. On my return home I went to bed. The doctor was sent for and he considered I was in a very weak state. But with his skill and the good nursing of my niece I was able to get about again within a month, but was not allowed to do any[Pg 211] public work for some time. But as the spring came along I grew stronger and was enabled to resume my public work, and late in the summer of 1919 the South Norfolk Divisional Labour Party sent me an invitation to contest the Division again in the Labour interest, as there was a rumour that the member's father, Lord Cozens-Hardy, was very ill and could not live long, and in that case there would have to be a bye-election since the member would be raised to the Peerage. I gave the matter very serious consideration. I consulted my doctor, and he considered it would be absolutely unsafe for me to undertake another parliamentary contest. I had already fresh local duties, for in the spring I was elected on the Fakenham Parish Council and was elected its chairman, and, further, not being able to accomplish my desire in 1918, namely to finish my life's work in the House of Commons, I had no further desire to enter Parliament, but was anxious to finish my life's work in doing local work. I therefore decided not to accept the invitation, but to leave that part of public work to younger men, and on September 23, 1919, I wrote declining the invitation in a letter to Mr. Gooch, the Party's honorary agent.

During the autumn of 1919 I addressed several meetings for the Union, and also devoted much time to local public work, the duties of which increased rapidly. My health improved and I gained a good deal of strength. The condition of my heart, however, caused the doctor a good deal of anxiety. The Divisional Labour Party decided that they would not let the seat go uncontested, and at a special meeting of the Party on May 29, 1920, passed a resolution asking the Labourers' Union again to find a candidate to contest the Division whenever the election took place. The Union had already taken a ballot for candidates for the next General Election. Accordingly they sent Mr. W. Holmes down to meet the Divisional Party. The Party had also asked for other nominations[Pg 212] besides asking the Union for a candidate, and the following persons were nominated: Mr. W. B. Taylor, Mr. T. G. Higdon, Mr. William G. Codling, and Mr. E. G. Gooch. Mr. Codling did not attend, and Mr. Gooch withdrew. Each of the other nominees addressed the delegates. I presided over the meeting. After each one of the men had given their views and been closely questioned, they were asked to retire, and, on the vote being taken, Mr. Taylor received 40 votes, Mr. Holmes 16, Mr. Higdon 1. Mr. Taylor was declared elected and, after a vote had been passed to me for presiding and Mr. Taylor had been finally endorsed, the meeting separated. Mr. Taylor at once commenced a campaign, and a subscription list was opened. He not being the Union's official candidate, the Union had no financial liability; in fact, they could not contribute to his fund. He made good progress, however, and the agent succeeded in raising several pounds, and I think if there had been no by-election by the time the General Election came they would have raised a very considerable sum. But Lord Cozens-Hardy died in June and a by-election had to take place. This found the Party altogether unprepared for the fight. A special meeting of the Party was called, and they decided to withdraw from the election and concentrate on the General Election. The other two political parties had selected their candidates. Mr. C. H. Roberts was standing for the Independent Liberals, and Mr. J. H. Batty was standing for the Coalition-Liberals, and both candidates had got their campaigns in full swing. The Liberal candidate was delighted at the withdrawal, and predicted that he would win. There was, however, a class of people who were not at all pleased at Labour not fighting, and they showed their displeasure by writing to the Executive of the Labourers' Union and demanding that they should put a candidate of their own into the field, threatening that if they did not they would leave the Union. The Executive decided to call[Pg 213] a conference of delegates from every branch of the Union in the Division at Wymondham. The Norfolk members of the Executive with the President attended the conference with power to act. They also decided to invite the Executive of the Divisional Labour Party to attend. The meeting was held in the Labour Institute. Every branch of the Union in the Division was represented. The President, in a lengthy speech, pointed out the difficulties, considering that the contest had already commenced and the writ been issued, and he invited the delegates to express their views. With one voice they requested that the Union should put a candidate into the field, many of the delegates declaring that, if we did not contest, their members would leave the Union. They were also unanimous in their view that the seat could be won for Labour. A resolution was moved that the Union be requested to put a candidate into the field and that the Executive of the Divisional Labour Party be invited to co-operate. This was carried with the greatest enthusiasm, everyone standing and cheering to the echo. Then the question was asked by the President who was to be the man, and the delegates at once said there was only one man that could fight and win, and that was "their George" (as they were so fond of calling me and as I like that they should). I pointed out to them my age and my weakness, which they would find a disadvantage to them in the contest. They said they would be prepared to meet that if I would but consent to stand, for with me they were sure they could win, and further, they would do all the work, and I should have nothing to trouble me but to speak at the meetings. With this promise I replied that if they could win the seat for Labour with me as their candidate, then I was at their service. This was received with loud cheering. All the ladies present volunteered at once for work in connection with issuing my address, etc. Mr. W. B. Taylor, J.P., C.C., who had retired[Pg 214] from the contest, at once volunteered to render all the help he could and promised to enter the fight with the same enthusiasm as if he had been the candidate. Mr. Edwin Gooch promised to undertake the honorary agency as before, and my dear friend, the President of the Union, Mr. W. R. Smith, who I am so fond of calling "My Boy," undertook to throw all his influence into the contest by addressing meetings and looking after me at the meetings and not allowing me to overtax my strength.

The press had got a hint that, after all, Labour was not going to let the seat go by default and that a meeting was being held for that purpose. They had, therefore, got their reporters to gather up the first information of what had taken place. But the public had not the slightest idea previously who would be the candidate, and were taken by surprise. The news was flashed over the wires to the furthest parts of the country. On the Monday morning the papers had great headlines: "George Edwards enters the Fight." Leading articles were written on the matter, all agreeing that I was the strongest local candidate Labour could bring into the field, and it became evident at once that there would be the greatest interest taken in the contest. It also created a great surprise in the camps of the two opposing political parties. After the conference was over I journeyed to Stow Bedon to attend a demonstration in connection with the Agricultural Labourers' Union at which I had been announced to speak. Here I made my first election speech, as we naturally turned this to some political account. The chairman, Mr. H. T. Phoenix, announced that I had that day been adopted as the Labour candidate. I was accompanied to this meeting by Mr. and Mrs. Gooch and a whole host of Wymondham friends. Mr. W. B. Taylor and the Rev. P. S. Carden, the esteemed minister of the Scott Memorial Church, Norwich, also spoke at this meeting. The meeting was most enthusiastic. After the meeting was over I journeyed back to Wymondham and[Pg 215] again made my home at Mr. and Mrs. Long's. Although the next day was Sunday, we were compelled to devote a large part of it to making arrangements. The election had already been in progress for over a week. We had therefore much ground to make up. A plan of campaign was mapped out and all arrangements made to commence the campaign the next day. My address was got ready to print the next day, and by the Tuesday it was published. On the Monday we opened the campaign at Hethersett and Little Melton. I had with me Mr. G. E. Hewitt, Mr. Long and Mr. E. A. Beck. Although the meetings were only announced that morning they were crowded and most enthusiastic. For some unaccountable reason I had a clear vision from the very first that we should win and I never lost heart, which was so different to the

General Election. The Liberals grew very angry at my appearance on the scene, as they said I could not possibly win and that I should let the Coalition candidate in. We pushed on, however, with great vigour. Helpers came forward in great numbers. The Earl of Kimberley again came forward as he had done at the General Election and helped in every way possible, rendering most valuable service during the contest. My address caused a great deal of discussion, as it embraced the entire programme of the Party. It was as follows:—

SOUTH NORFOLK PARLIAMENTARY BYE-ELECTION.

Tuesday, July 27th, 1920.

To the Electors.

Ladies and Gentlemen,

Owing to the lamented death of Lord Cozens-Hardy and the elevation of the Hon. W. H. Cozens-Hardy to the Peerage, a vacancy has occurred in this Division. At the unanimous request of the branches of the National Agricultural Labourers' Union in South Norfolk, endorsed by the Divisional and National Labour Parties, I have consented to stand as Labour candidate for the Division and have pleasure in submitting the following statements of my principles and policy.

[Pg 216]

The Present Government and High Prices.

Although the Government has been in office for more than eighteen months nothing has been done to reduce the cost of living, which presses so hardly on all classes of the population. Every housewife knows prices still tend in an upward direction. The only policy likely to affect prices is the Labour policy of a strict limitation of profits, stringent control and nationalization. I strongly condemn the policy of waste of the present Government.

National Finance.

The war having left a huge burden of debt on the country amounting to over 8,000 million pounds, it will be easily recognized that this constitutes a terrible menace to the trade of the country and to the earning capacity in real wages of the workers. I advocate a levy of the fortunes of the wealthy people in preference to the taxing of the food and other necessities of the workers. Those who have made huge profits out of the sorrow and suffering of war should be compelled to disgorge this wealth, and so relieve the nation of a burden which will otherwise be too heavy to sustain.

Mines, Railways, Etc.

I shall support all reasonable efforts to secure for the nation the public ownership of all key services, such as mines, railways, canals, shipping, transport and the supply of power.

Foreign Policy.

The foreign policy of the Government stands condemned. I favour the establishment of a league of free peoples, peace with Russia, open diplomacy and self-determination for all nations, including Ireland.

Agriculture.

The Labour Party's policy for agriculture is based upon the national ownership of land. Agriculture must become the first consideration of the State. A standard living wage, a statutory working week, and the abolition of the tied cottage would enable the land worker to enjoy equally with other workers opportunities for individual recreation and development. Land for small holdings must be obtained easily and cheaply, and co-operation amongst small holders assisted and developed.

Security of Tenure.

If the land is to be brought back into a proper state of cultivation and be made to produce all the food it is capable of, then[Pg 217] the farmer must have security of tenure. I should, however, insist on proper cultivation of land and the employment of a sufficient number of efficient labourers to do so. In order to enforce this I should place even more drastic power in the hands of the Agricultural Councils than they now possess.

Elevation of Womanhood.

I am in favour of the immediate establishment of a pensions scheme for all widows with dependent children; the endowment of motherhood and the extension of the franchise to women as it is or may be granted to men.

Housing Question.

The prompt carrying through of a comprehensive national measure of housing, the local authorities being everywhere required to make good the whole of the existing shortage in well-planned, well-built, commodious and healthy homes for the entire population, assisted by National Exchequer grants sufficient in amount to prevent any charge falling on the local rates.

Unemployment and the Right to Work.

I should use every endeavour to secure the right to work for all. Industry must be organized to provide for opportunities of service for all. Failing such a system full maintenance must be guaranteed by the State. I favour drastic amendments to the Insurance Acts.

Ex-Service Men.

The Government have treated the sailors and soldiers and their dependants with meanness. The Labour Party is pledged to just and generous treatment to all ex-service men with regard to pensions, medical and surgical treatment, reinstatement in civil employment at Trade Union rates of wages, and complete security against involuntary unemployment. Owing to the rising cost of living I should press for an immediate increase on present pension rates.

Old Age Pensions.

There must be such a revision of pension rates and ages for eligibility for old age pensions as would enable the recipients to live in decency and comfort.

Conclusion.

I appeal, as a Norfolk man, for your support on the grounds of the long public service I have rendered to the people by my[Pg 218] work on many public authorities, especially during the last five years. Should you do me the honour of returning me as your member I will continue to work in this new sphere in the interests of the great toiling masses to which I belong, and in whose interests all the best years of my life have been given.

Yours very sincerely,
George Edwards.

Wymondham,
July 1920.

P.S.—I cannot hope to get round before polling day to every town and village, but I do beg every working man and woman to go to the poll and vote against the waste of the Government and the high cost of living. It is the only lesson to which they will listen.

I kept to my programme all through the campaign. One amusing tribute was paid to me at one of my opponent's (Mr. Batty's) meetings by one of his supporters, Major Kennedy, who said I was as good a fellow as ever walked. But he was anxious about me for, if I was elected, I should feel so out of place having to wear a frock coat and silk top hat. Another amusing thing happened. One of the lady canvassers for my opponent, anxious to enhance the cause of her candidate, said I was a dear old man, but it would be cruel to send me to Parliament at my age. All this, however, although not intended, was to my interest and, as the election day drew near, our people became more enthusiastic and my opponents began to realize that they had not got so easy a job as they had anticipated. The Independent Liberals kept encouraging their supporters by declaring they were sure they were winning; in fact, the night before the poll one of their speakers declared at Watton that they had won. They counted their chickens before they were hatched. The night before the poll our meetings were attended by hundreds and speakers flocked to our platform. At Attleborough we had Mr. J. Mills, M.P., and other local speakers. Mr. W. S. Royce, M.P., Lord Kimberley and Mr. Smith, M.P., were at Wymondham,[Pg 219] and held the fort until I arrived. My old friend and constant companion during the contest, Mr. G. E. Hewitt, J.P., C.C., accompanied me to my meetings. I spoke with him at three meetings. We made our way to Great Hockham and addressed a large meeting there, and then on to Attleborough, where we met with a tremendous reception. In this place at the General Election I could scarcely get a hearing.

My opponent, Mr. Batty, was also holding a meeting at the same place, but out of respect for me, on my arrival he adjourned his meeting until I had spoken and left the meeting and came and stood amongst my audience. Having spoken there I made my way to Wymondham. On arriving at the town I was met by the band of the Discharged Soldiers' and Sailors' Federation and a large number of my supporters, who played me up to the Fairland, the place of meeting, where there were upwards of 1,500 people waiting to receive me, and I was given a wonderful reception.

On the polling day my agent, Mr. Gooch, Mr. W. B. Taylor and I set out for a tour through the constituency. All went well until we arrived at Shotesham Common, when the motor broke down. Here we had to wait at this lonely spot for three hours until another motor arrived, when we renewed our journey. Everywhere we went we were received with the greatest enthusiasm. We found our colour (green) most prominent. That was the colour I had adopted, being the colour of the Union. On our return to Wymondham we were met by crowds. We found the Earl of Kimberley hard at work with his motor gaily trimmed with our colour. He had also put two waggons on the road to fetch up distant voters. Mr. Royce, M.P., had lent us his motor, which rendered us splendid service. At the close of the poll our people were confident we had won. They assembled at the Labour Institute, where a most enthusiastic meeting was held. The next day I returned to my home to wait[Pg 220] patiently until August 9th, when the votes were to be counted. I was confident, however, that we had won. The whole contest was most pleasant. Everyone seemed so confident and worked with such good will and hope. I look back to this contest with the most pleasant memories. I am afraid there was a good deal of betting about the result, not amongst my supporters, but amongst the outside people.

[Pg 221]

CHAPTER XVIII
PARLIAMENT

The votes were counted at the Shirehouse, Norwich, on Monday August 9th. My niece and I were early astir and we decorated ourselves with the party colour. My neighbour presented me with a little toy black cat for luck. Another sent me a small horseshoe.

On arriving at the Shirehouse I found my agent and my close friend, Mr. W. R. Smith, all smiles and in close conversation, as the counting had been proceeding some time before my arrival. One of the other candidates had arrived before me, Mr. C. H. Roberts with Lady Roberts. Soon after my arrival the other candidate, Mr. Batty, arrived, and we three gave each other the usual friendly greeting. By a quarter to one it was evident I was well ahead and that it was not possible that either of the other candidates could win. About a quarter to two the counting was completed and the High Sheriff announced the figures.

It will be seen by the figures that Mr. Batty, the Co.-Liberal, did not receive as many votes by sixty as I did at the General Election. Thus there was a great turnover in public opinion against the Government, for if you add Mr. Roberts' total to mine, it makes a majority of over five thousand against the Government. After the figures were given the High Sheriff announced them outside, and there was a cheer from my supporters whom I briefly thanked.

[Pg 222]

The figures were as follows:—

George Edwards   8,594
J. H. Batty (Co.-Lib.)   6,476
C. H. Roberts (Free Lib.)   3,718
———

   Labour majority   2,118

The following is a press report of the speeches after the declaration:—

The customary vote of thanks was moved inside the Council Chamber by Mr. Edwards. He spoke of the Acting Returning Officer as a most impartial, kind, and painstaking officer. As for my opponents, he went on, we have had a most pleasant contest. I do not think any one of the three has said a word or done anything that he would have to regret. When the General Election comes Labour cannot wish to have more honourable opponents than it has met on this occasion. This victory that we have secured is not a personal victory. It has been won by a noble band of men and women who have done their best to win success for the principles they hold dear. I shall be loyal to the principles that these noble men and women have fought for.

Mr. Batty seconded the motion. They were all most grateful to the Returning Officer and his staff, and they hoped for Mr. Edwards' sake it might be a long time before there was another election in South Norfolk. He added: It was a personal pleasure to me to be able to congratulate Mr. Edwards. It was not until this morning that I had the pleasure of shaking his hand. I cannot but feel that in some respects Mr. Edwards' opinion is not quite correct. I am inclined to think that the result is somewhat of a personal tribute to his lifelong work in the constituency. I congratulate him, and I am sure my friend Mr. Roberts joins with me in this respect on his thus receiving the crown of his life's work, and I hope he may be spared long to enjoy it.

Mr. Roberts, in supporting the motion, said he agreed with Mr. Edwards that the contest had been fought fairly and without bitterness. He gladly took the opportunity of offering Mr. Edwards his personal congratulations. The result of the election must be a satisfaction to Mr. Edwards, not only because it meant a victory for his principles, but because it was a mark of the esteem and confidence of his friends and neighbours.

The Acting Returning Officer made a brief reply.

[Pg 223]

In the course of a press interview after the declaration I said:—

Labour has won a splendid victory. I do not look upon this result as a personal tribute, but as a victory for Labour principles, and a warning to the Government to clear out and make room for those who will run the country better. This is practically the first agricultural constituency in England to return a Labour member to Parliament, and I shall be the second bona fide agricultural representative to sit in the House. The first was Joe Arch, with whom I worked in the old days.

After the poll was declared I returned to Wymondham, where I found a large number of telegrams awaiting me, and at seven o'clock a large number gathered at the Fairland Hall to hold a congratulation meeting. I returned home to Fakenham in the morning, where I found another large batch of telegrams waiting. I also received numbers of letters of congratulation, many of them from my political opponents.

On Tuesday August 11th I attended the funeral of the late Mr. Sancroft Holmes (Chairman of the Norfolk County Council) who a few days before had died in my presence at Holkham Hall when attending an Advisory Committee for the nomination of magistrates for the County of Norfolk, of which we were both members. My niece and I both returned to Wymondham that night in readiness to proceed to London the next day for me to take my seat.

On Wednesday morning we were early astir ready for our journey. From the Monday to the Wednesday morning I had not really realized that I was actually a Member of Parliament. It was brought home to me, however, when I had to get ready to proceed to London, and then, strange as it may seem, instead of my being full of joy, I actually broke down with the deepest emotion. I cannot account for it, but it was so, and the first words that I could utter were a desire that my poor dear wife could know. I also offered a fervent prayer that God[Pg 224] would keep me humble and that I might always remain the same George Edwards, the agricultural labourer. This might appear to be approaching very near to cant, but it was sincere and I have tried to live it out.

A little band left Wymondham by the 9 a.m. train. I was accompanied by my faithful agent Mr. Gooch and Mrs. Gooch, Mr. W. B. Taylor, Mr. J. Smith (Secretary of the Wymondham Local Labour Party) and Mrs. Smith and my niece, Mrs. Kernick. We arrived at Liverpool Street Station a little after 12 a.m. and were due at the House of Commons at two o'clock. At the House we found Mr. W. R. Smith waiting for us in the outer lobby, but before we reached the House we were caught by several camera men. Tickets for the gallery had been secured by Mr. Smith for my friends to enable them to witness me walk up the House and take the oath. Punctually at a quarter to four, after question time, the Speaker asked the usual question on these occasions—if there were any new members desirous of taking their seats? Then came the ordeal. Accompanied by Mr. Smith and the late Mr. Tyson Wilson, who was Chief Whip of the Labour Party at the time, I walked up to the clerk's table and took the oath and signed the Roll Book and shook hands with the Speaker and then took my seat amidst the cheers of my friends, one singing "The Farmer's Boy." My friend Mr. Smith said it was the proudest day of his life when he conducted me up the House. Such is the close friendship that exists between us.

A peculiar incident happened when I signed the book. In my nervousness I had one of my feet lifted up, and the Premier, Mr. Lloyd George, unconsciously put his foot underneath mine, and when I placed my foot down I put it on to his. I have since joked him concerning the incident several times.

After a few minutes my friends and I went down on to the terrace and had tea, and the first to come and[Pg 225] congratulate me was my first opponent, Lord Cozens-Hardy.

I stayed in London until the Friday when I returned to Wymondham. On the Saturday I went to Norwich and attended to my County Council Committee work, where I received most hearty congratulations from my colleagues on the Council. But a greater surprise was awaiting me on my return to Fakenham in the evening. Arriving at the Great Eastern Station by the quarter to eight train I found waiting for me a large number of my fellow townsmen of all shades of political thought, the Fakenham Town Band and a conveyance to take me to the Market Square. This was drawn by hand. I was practically lifted into the conveyance and by my side was my little adopted child. The band headed the procession and played "See the Conquering Hero Comes." The streets were lined with spectators and when the Market Square was reached there were crowds waiting to give me a reception. It was considered that there were over two thousand people present. The conveyance was drawn into the square and a congratulation speech was made by my friend Mr. Robert Watson. Mr. Walker of the Printers' Union presided and addresses were also given by Mr. H. Allen and others. I thanked the people for the kind reception they had given me, which was the greatest joy of my life, to receive such a welcome by my neighbours in my own native town. A full report of the affair was given in the Eastern Daily Press on the Monday with some very nice comments. The report was headed "The Warrior's Return."

The House adjourned on Monday August 16th and I settled down for my well-earned rest, but the request from the Christian Churches to conduct special religious services was greater than I could possibly comply with. As soon as harvest operations were completed and I had had a nice rest I took a tour through my constituency and thanked my supporters for the support they had given to[Pg 226] the noble cause of Labour. I was received everywhere with the greatest kindness and enthusiasm.

On October 19th the House reassembled for the Autumn Session, and I returned to London to attend to my duties, and on October 21st there was a debate on the unemployment question. I followed the Minister of Labour and made my maiden speech as follows:—

I have listened very attentively to the speech of the right hon. gentleman. I am not so much concerned with the description he gave us of the state of unemployment as I am with the fact that there are unemployed and a lack of provision made for them to find employment—especially among ex-service men. I find that my right hon. friend is very anxious to lay the responsibility for the unemployment and the lack of provision for the unemployed upon everyone except the Government. He dealt with the housing question, and he made a great point of the fact that housing is being delayed in consequence of the conduct of the Trade Unionists in the building industry. But he did not tell the House that the Trade Union workers in the trade offered that if the Government will guarantee there shall be no unemployed in their trade they will remove the restrictions of which he complains. The point I want to come to is this—the delay in erecting houses for ex-service men and for the working class in this country lies at the door of the Government. What are the facts? I speak with some knowledge. The Minister of Health, or the Government through him, pressed on the local authorities the responsibility of providing houses under the Act, and I say without hesitation that the local authorities—and all credit is due to them—undertook that responsibility. It has become notorious how their action has been defeated. Take my own area.

We decided to erect 350 houses. We prepared our plans and put out our contracts. We erected a number of houses for the working classes. We were told by the Government that in deciding on the rents we were to fix such a rent as we deemed reasonable according to wages earned in the district. We fixed the rents, as some of us think, rather too high. We had full local knowledge. We said that for a six-roomed house the rent should be £20 per year, with the rates on top of that, and for a five-roomed house £14 per year, plus rates. What did the Minister of Health do? We sent him a return showing that the earnings of the agricultural labourers in the district averaged £2 6s. per week, and those of other classes of workers £3 10s. per[Pg 227] week. The Minister came down on top of us and would not sanction the rents we had fixed. He demanded that the local authority should charge a man earning £3 10s. per week £1 per week as rent, and that for the five-roomed house 16s. 6d. per week should be charged. Do the Government imagine that any local authority, with its knowledge of the condition of things, would be content to erect houses and to ask agricultural labourers with their wives and families to pay a rent of 16s. 6d. per week out of a wage of £2 6s.? Do they imagine that any local authority will erect houses for which they are to charge a man earning £3 10s. per week £1 as rent? Do they imagine that out of the wages they are earning the men could pay such high rents as that? If they do, I can only suggest they should experiment on themselves for one month at least. This bombshell was thrown at the local authorities throughout the length and breadth of the country, with the result that they will not touch housing schemes until the Minister of Health abates his demands in this respect. I maintain that the responsibility for the delay in erecting houses falls directly upon the Government, but for whose action house-building might have been proceeded with, and the present unemployment would not have grown to the extent it has. Then there is the question of raw material. The Government were warned in 1918—in the early part of that year—that there would be a terrible shortage of raw material and especially of bricks. Labour Exchanges sent resolution after resolution urging the Government to take steps to reopen the brickfields which had gone into disuse during the war. We were laughed at for our efforts in pointing out that there must be a terrible shortage unless something in this direction was done. Remember, the unskilled men now waiting for training might have been put on this work, and the necessary raw material could have been provided without difficulty. What happened? Those local authorities which had contracts in hand found that the men had to stand idle for the lack of raw material. I was very much interested in a speech made by the Minister of Health in regard to the agricultural industry. I have a knowledge of this industry. I was engaged in it for many years, and I remember the time when there were 950,000 agricultural labourers and others employed on the land. At the present time there are only 550,000 so employed, and yet we have in my own county to-day 500 agricultural labourers standing by for want of work! I heard a question asked of the Minister of Health why this was so. I think I can give the reply. It is largely due to the gambling which is now going on in land. It is also due, in part, to the bad farming which has been prevalent for many years. That is responsible for the great decrease in the number of men employed on the land. We ask[Pg 228] the Government, as far as the land question is concerned, to do what they did during the war, namely to put into force the compulsory clauses of the Defence of the Realm Act. We have to-day, I believe, between 2,000,000 and 3,000,000 acres of land out of cultivation. We were told the other day that there were 800,000 acres less under wheat this year, and I believe I am correct in saying that since the Armistice 80,000 acres of land have gone out of cultivation that were brought under cultivation during the war. Why do not the Government put into force the compulsory clauses, and compel those who call the land theirs to keep it in cultivation? Something has been said about afforestation. In my own county we have something like 3,000 acres of land that is useful for that purpose. I do not say, with my knowledge of agriculture, that all the land is suitable for producing food; I know it is not; but it will produce something that the nation wants. That land is now lying derelict. It is only used as rabbit warrens, because it pays the landlord better to keep it for game preserving than it does to produce things that we want. If the Government would step in, and I appeal to them to do so, they could at once set to work most of this unskilled labour—we are told that it would require no skill—if they would insist upon the use of this land for this purpose. I know that it is suitable for the production of wood, which is greatly needed.

The Government were forewarned of these things. They know that this land is there ready to produce something. Indeed, I would venture to state that there is not an acre of land in this country which does not produce something that the nation needs. All that is necessary is that the people should have an opportunity of getting on the land. With regard to the Land Settlement scheme, as a County Councillor I have had something to do with putting this Act into force. What are the facts? We were told that there were £8,000,000 set aside for this purpose. So far as my County Council is concerned—and I think we stand second in the country for putting the Small Holdings and Allotments Act into force—we were told that we were to have this money to purchase land. What does the Land Settlement Act do? It compels us to give inflated prices for the land, and, having given inflated prices—not pre-war value, but war-profit value, the price to which it has been run up in the market by the land gamblers—we are compelled to charge these ex-service men, these heroes who have fought our battles, and who were told by the Prime Minister that they should have a land fit for heroes to live in, where no inhabitants should ever hunger—we have to charge them a rent that we know full well they will never be able to pay and get a living. The Government come along and say: "Yes, we will lend you money, but will charge you 6 per cent. for it,"[Pg 229] and we have to charge that back to these poor fellows. In my own county we have 500 ex-service men who cannot get on the land, and we have spent all the money the Government will let us have. I would make an appeal to the right hon. gentleman opposite and to the Government to take this question seriously. I have spent fifty years of my life trying to upraise my class. I have endeavoured to exercise a moderating influence, and I think that up to the present I have been successful. No one can charge me with being an extremist. I want, however, to point this out to the Government. Our influence over men and women may be lessened when they know that the barns are full and the cupboard is empty. Therefore I ask them to use all the powers they possess under the Defence of the Realm Act and to deal at once with this land problem. It can be dealt with at once. Set these men to work. We do not plead for doles; we do not plead for charity. What we say is: "In Heaven's name, find them work!"

During the Autumn Session I never left the House nor missed a Division. In the middle of November the Agricultural Bill was brought before the House on its report stage. This received my whole-hearted support in all its stages and I spoke several times when it was before the House. With my friends Mr. Royce and Mr. Smith I tried to improve it by moving new clauses from the point of view of giving the labourer who lived in a tied cottage some security in his home and, after several interviews with Sir Arthur Boscawen, the Minister who had charge of the Bill, we were able to make a little improvement by securing to the labourers compensation in the shape of a year's rent and expenses of removal if compelled to leave his cottage at short notice. We also secured to the tenant farmer some security of tenure or compensation for disturbance and we also secured a minimum price for his corn and the re-establishment of the Wage Board for four years, which alas! was so soon to be abolished by the repeal of the Agricultural Act of 1921.

During the passage of the Agricultural Act we had many late nights. The last days of the sitting, December 20th and 21st, I never left the House for thirty-six hours[Pg 230] and went into the Division Lobby nearly thirty times against the Lords Amendments. This concluded my first experience of the House of Commons.

Soon after my entrance into Parliament I was asked to become a member of the Industrial Christian Fellowship, an association established by leaders of the Church of England for the purpose of bringing our industrial system more into harmony with the principles taught by Christ Himself and further of endeavouring to create a higher spiritual life in the great Labour movement and preventing it from becoming too materialistic. As that had been my ideal all through my long public life, it at once appealed to me, and I decided to accept the invitation to become a member of the General Council. The first meeting I attended and addressed was at Hull. Before going, however, I expressed a wish to meet members of the Trades and Labour Council. A meeting was arranged and I found there was a suspicion amongst the Trade Unionists in the city that there was some ulterior motive behind it. I endeavoured to dispel this suspicion. My address was entitled "The High Ideals of the Labour Movement." The large hall was full and the Mayor presided.

In November of the same year (1920) I received an invitation from Canon Newson to give an address in Newcastle-on-Tyne Cathedral on December 5th. I accepted the invitation and at Newcastle was met at the station by Canon Newson with whom I stayed the week-end. During the afternoon I was introduced to the Bishop with whom I had a long talk on the religious aspect of the movement. In the evening I met members of the Trades and Labour Council at the Canon's House. On Sunday afternoon I gave my address on "Religion and Labour" in the cathedral.

This address was listened to with marked attention by a large congregation. The fact that a layman and a prominent Nonconformist had been invited to give an[Pg 231] address in a cathedral had created widespread interest. Many of the daily papers gave a long report of my address. Since then I have spoken in two churches in London on "National Righteousness." This I think is a sign that there is a great awakening in the social consciousness of the people and that a spirit of fellowship and goodwill is abroad such as has never been manifested before. I consider that I have never been connected with a movement that was calculated to bring our industrial and social life on to a higher platform and I wish it God-speed in its good work.

In February 1921 I was invited by His Majesty the King to an afternoon garden party at Buckingham Palace, and on my being introduced to the King and His Majesty ascertaining that I came from Norfolk, he expressed a wish to have a few minutes' talk with me. His Majesty asked me concerning my early life, also the condition of the people in Norfolk. The matter was given publicity through the press and the following appeared in one paper:—

By invitation of their Majesties the King and Queen, Mr. George Edwards, M.P., attended the afternoon party at Buckingham Palace last Thursday. Mr. Edwards had the honour of being presented to their Majesties, and during the afternoon the King expressed a wish to have some further conversation with the member for South Norfolk, to whom His Majesty directed inquiries respecting his early days. The King evinced deep interest in the story Mr. Edwards told, and later the Queen also invited the member to relate to her the story of his early struggles.

After cordially greeting Mr. Edwards, the King said he was interested to know that he came from Norfolk, and inquired if the member was a native of this county. His Majesty also inquired what occupation Mr. Edwards' father followed.

The remarkable story of the member's progress from workhouse to Westminster greatly interested the King, who plied Mr. Edwards with questions relative to his early life.

Mr. Edwards told His Majesty that he was a native of Norfolk, and that his father, like himself, was an agricultural labourer. "At the time of my birth," said Mr. Edwards, "the wages of the agricultural labourer were 8s. a week, and at the time of the [Pg 232] Crimean War in 1854 the cost of living rose to its highest, but the wages of the labourer remained stationary."

"And how did you fare?" inquired the King.

"My father and mother had to undergo the greatest privations," Mr. Edwards replied. "We never had bread enough and the family were fed largely on turnips which my father brought from his master's field. At five years of age I was a workhouse boy."

"And this was really the way you lived?" exclaimed the King.

His Majesty was obviously touched by the account given him and expressed the deepest sympathy.

"One of my own labourers," said the King, "brought up a family on 13s. a week, but this is much worse. How were you educated?"

"I never went to school in my life," said the member. "My wife first taught me to read, and I put myself in a position to purchase books by giving up the luxury of tobacco."

His Majesty asked as to the welfare of the labourers to-day and inquired if they were better off?

"Yes, decidedly," replied Mr. Edwards, "but there is a good deal of privation now."

The conversation then turned to the position of affairs on His Majesty's Norfolk estate at Sandringham, the King suggesting that working conditions there were satisfactory.

Mr. Edwards agreed, and said he desired to express the greatest appreciation of the efforts of the King in regard to working conditions at Sandringham. "If all other landlords followed along the same lines," added Mr. Edwards, "there would be little trouble."

The King expressed his best wishes for Mr. Edwards' future.

Mr. Edwards had several minutes' conversation with the Queen, who gave further proof of her interest in the housing of the people. Her Majesty referred to housing conditions at Sandringham, and Mr. Edwards expressed appreciation of what had been done for the labourers on the estate with regard to housing, and remarked that everything had been done that it was possible to do for the home comforts of the tenants.

This brings my story almost to a close.

During my time I have seen what amounts almost to a revolution in the lives of the people. There is no comparison between the life of the village worker when I was a lad and now. I have seen one Trade Union spring up and fall. But during its short life, under the leadership[Pg 233] of Joseph Arch, George Rix, Z. Walker and others, it did some wonderful work for the agricultural workers. Through its influence the labourers were enfranchised. The District and Parish Council Act was put in force, and I look back with pleasure at the humble part I was able to take in this matter. Many years after that, as stated above, I founded the present Union, and I have lived to see it spread from Norfolk into every county in England and Wales. It has gone from a little back-room of mine in a little cottage in which I lived at Gresham to a fine block of buildings at 72, Acton Street, London. It has accomplished much for the agricultural labourers. It has entirely altered and brightened up the monotonous life of the labourer. It has given him a broader outlook on life and I hope he will let nothing separate him from the Union that has in so short a time done so much for him, his wife and children.

As in the days of Arch there is again another attempt to divide our forces by introducing what they call a New Union. This is being done by those who ought to have known better. Are the labourers going to let history repeat itself? If so, then all the sacrifice I have made and the years of labour I have given on their behalf will be thrown away. No, I cannot believe they will. I have too strong a faith in their good common sense and in their devotion and gratitude towards those who laboured so hard for them to be led away by the platitudes of some new-born friends.

In presenting my readers with my life-story let me ask them, especially the young readers, as they read it to watch carefully my limitations and failings (and they will detect many), to study them attentively, and in starting out in life to try and avoid them. Also, whatever they may see in the story that is worthy to be followed, let them try to follow it. They are starting life now, thank God, under much better circumstances than I did.

[Pg 234]

As they read the facts here related they will notice a touch of sadness running through it all. They will also notice the many bitter struggles I have had coming along this somewhat rugged road of life; how I have battled to lift myself above my environment; how I have laboured to educate myself and to inform myself on all public questions, and I hope they will also detect a burning desire from the first to use the knowledge I had obtained for the benefit of my own class, as I hope, with some amount of success. They will, I trust, gather from the early pages of this story that the sufferings of my parents and the privations that they underwent for their children had branded themselves on my soul like a hot iron and that from my very early days I became determined to do all I could to make the life of my own class much brighter and better than it was in those dark days.

As I look back on the years of the past and the events in my life I am mystified. I cannot understand what has been the overruling power in my life. As the reader will see, disappointments have been my lot over and over again. Many times in the hour of disappointment, smarting under what I felt to be the ingratitude of the class for whom I made so much sacrifice, I have said I could never again make any attempt to help them. Yet as often as I have said that some overpowering force compelled me to re-enter the field.

There is, however, a secret behind all this and a reason for the success that has crowned my labours although late in life. First the loving and devoted wife it was my fortune to have. Never on any occasion, whatever her own feelings might be, did she sound one despondent note; but in my hours of depression would always give me a word of encouragement. Although her death cast a great sadness on my life, yet at the opportune moment there was light in the darkness, for at her death her niece, Mrs. Kenrick, who is so much like her in character and, if it could be[Pg 235] possible, even more sympathetic, offered to come and look after me as she has done for these last ten years. She has entered into all my public life and has made my life brighter than it could otherwise have been and made the road to success much easier.

Another cause of the success in my life has been the strong character I have been able to build up by embracing Christian principles and my strong faith in the great sacrificial life of Christ who gave His life for the cause of humanity. It has enabled me to put my best into everything I have taken in hand, and I would like to impress upon my readers that in my opinion that is the only true road to success in life. I am sure it has been the real cause of my being able to accomplish what I have in the cause to which I have devoted so much of my life.

Amidst all the turmoil of my public life I have remained true to my first faith and have been loyal to the first Church of my choice, the Primitive Methodist, and filled most of the offices open to laymen in connection with that Church. This I would recommend to my readers as being the one essential thing: whatever our convictions may be, to be true to them.

I can truly say that has been my one impelling motive and is what I have always aimed at, to be true to my conscience. I never entered into anything until I had assured myself it was right and, when once I had done that, nothing whatever could turn me from the path of duty.

Sometimes the members of my own Church could not quite understand me. One point in connection with my public work on which I have differed from them is the holding of labour meetings on Sundays. They hold strong convictions that such meetings are not paying due reverence to the Sunday as we ought to. I was some long time before I came to any other conclusion and refused to take any part in Sunday labour meetings. I thought the matter out very seriously for myself, however, and at last I came to the conclusion that the Labour movement was built[Pg 236] on the very rock of Christianity and that I was as much serving God by preaching what I believed to be the gospel of God, namely economic freedom, as when I occupied the pulpit. When, however, responsible for arranging such meetings I would insist upon them being conducted on strictly religious lines. I again ask my young readers to stand by their convictions, think out matters for themselves and, once convinced they are right, go straight forward. But above all to be true to God and your brother man is the only road to success.

The great human progress that has been made during this past seventy years, especially in the lives of the agricultural labourers, in which I have been able to take some humble part, is marvellous. Seventy years ago the village labourer was a mere chattel in the industrial world. His children were badly fed and uneducated.

The labourer had no voice in his local affairs. He had no vote. He was compelled to accept such conditions as were offered him and dared not complain. If he did so, he was a marked man. Now we have obtained for him collective bargaining and through his organizations he has a voice in all local authorities. This has worked a wonderful change. He has his vote and is now qualified to be even a Justice of the Peace. Both men and women have already been appointed. Many of the old colleagues that helped to bring about this change have passed away. In fact, I am the only one left to take any active part in public movements of those that worked with the late Joseph Arch, the founder of the first Union in 1872. Many of them died before they saw accomplished what they had set themselves out to do. But other men are reaping where they have sowed. I have seen the first Unions come and go and with their fall the labourer set back. And in 1906 I founded the greatest Union and, as will be seen by this story, it was built up by hard work and at great sacrifice by others besides myself, to whom the men owe a great debt of[Pg 237] gratitude. Some of these worthy men I will name: Mr. G. E. Hewitt, Mr. J. A. Arnett, Mr. W. Holmes, Mr. T. G. Higdon, the late Mr. Robert Green, and lastly my dear and closest friend, Mr. W. R. Smith M.P., the President of the Union, upon whose shoulders the brunt of the Union's work is at the moment. I ought also to say that I could not possibly have done what I did at the early stages of the Union had it not have been for the financial help I received from my friends the Earl of Kimberley and Mr. Herbert Day of Norwich. Now the one great question that weighs upon my mind is this: Are the men for whom I spent my life going to maintain the position that has been won for them? The position is not without danger. As in the days of Mr. Arch, so now there are forces working to divide the men and to spread distrust amongst them if they succeed. There is a danger of much that has been gained being lost. I have, however, great faith in the cause of democracy and there is still a brighter day to come for the men in our country-side. I may not live to see it. My last word of this story to my colleagues and to the young men is to work on in your good cause, to be reasonable and just, and to let the spirit of moderation and goodwill dwell amongst you.

> Oh! droop not though pain, sin and anguish be round thee
> Bravely fling off the gold chain that hath bound thee.
> Look to clear Heaven shining above thee.
> Rest not content in thy darkness a clod.
> Work for some good, be it ever so slowly.
> Labour, all labour, is noble and holy.
> Let thy great deeds be thy prayer to God.

Printed in Great Britain
by Amazon